DAMON

Living A Dream

LIFE IN THE LIMELIGHT

By DAMON BAILEY

With Wendell Trogdon

Backroads Press

Distributed by Damon Bailey Enterprises
Post Office Box 1510
Bedford, IN 47421

and

Backroads Press
P.O. Box 651
Mooresville, IN 46158

ISBN 0-9642371-2-1

Cover by Gary Varvel

Printed by
Country Pines Printing
Shoals, Indiana

To Mom, Dad, Courtney and Stacey

for all their love and inspiration

ACKNOWLEDGMENTS

A number of relatives and friends helped make this book possible. I cannot name all of them, but I am grateful for their assistance. I do want to thank Mom and Dad, Stacey, Courtney and Aunt Nancy Bailey. I also am appreciative of the cooperation of Ray Housel, my advisor; Tom Taylor, my AAU coach; Dan Bush, my high school coach; sports editor Bob Bridge of the *Bedford Times-Mail*, and photographers Mike Fender, Rich Miller and Joe Vitti.

FOREWORD

"Damon is so popular because he fulfills the myth of the All-American who reaches that level with hard work and sheer will. He is living proof that you do not have to be 7 feet tall or be a great leaper to be a great basketball player. People can relate to him."

—Ron Newlin, former executive director
Indiana High School Basketball Hall of Fame

* * *

"Damon Bailey is not the best shooter in the world. He is not the best rebounder. He is not the best passer. He is not the best defensive player. He is not the best dribbler. He is, however, good in all facets of the game. He is a complete player and that is what has made him great."

—Indiana Lt. Gov. Frank O'Bannon,
before Damon's final home game at I.U.

* * *

We were talking basketball as usual at the Heltonville alumni reunion one night in the mid-1980s when "Herbie" Harrell asked, "Have you heard about this kid, Damon Bailey?"

Bailey and basketball were synonymous around the southern Indiana town, had been for decades, but we were not familiar with Damon. "Wendell's son, Jesse's grandson," explained Harrell as he sketched a family tree.

"Keep an eye on him," Harrell suggested, mentioning he had seen Damon play on the unbeaten grade school team, was impressed at his ability and court awareness.

"It's a long way from May to December," we replied, knowing that the future is uncertain, that the road to greatness sometimes is marked by unexpected detours.

Harrell, however, had been around Heltonville for decades, had kept score at games until the local high school became part of the Bedford North Lawrence consolidation. He knew basketball and we respected his opinion so we stored his prediction in our memory bank.

Time passed. Some time later a reporter at *The Indianapolis News* suggested we call to the computer screen an Associated Press story about "some kid from Heltonville." That kid was Damon Bailey and he had scored the winning basket to lead his Amateur Athletic Union team to a national championship.

It was his first brush with national attention. It would not be his last. In the years that followed, Damon Bailey remained on the road marked "Great Expectations" by the "Herbie" Harrells of Heltonville.

Damon was by then an eighth grader at Shawswick and it was time to see if he was as good as he was touted to be. He was. He could dunk, palm the ball, score, rebound and play defense. It was obvious he was advanced beyond his age.

We no longer were skeptics. Neither was Indiana coach Bob Knight who twice made the pilgrimage to Shawswick later that season.

Over the next four years at Bedford North Lawrence High School, Damon would become a folk hero, admired by fans, respected by opponents, appreciated by coaches. He was first team all-state each year, a member of a state championship team, Mr. Basketball, the state's all time high school scorer.

His picture appeared on the covers of magazines, his exploits reported in newspapers from New York to Los Angeles, his fame stretching beyond the imagination of his earliest admirers.

Through it all he remained Damon, the quiet kid who would rather call attention to his coaches and his teammates than himself. He did not shun publicity, but he shared it. He remained immune from the conceit that often accompanies attention.

He had become larger than life to some Indiana University fans who awaited his arrival with unrealistic goals. They expected a super-scorer. They received a team player, one willing to sacrifice personal glory for the good of the team.

Life at I.U. was no plateau. It had peaks and valleys. Big days, great nights, 30-plus point games. Off-days, sore muscles, tendinitis, hip pointers. Good days followed bad, bringing more triumphs than defeats.

When it was over, he had proved he was a complete player, an all-American. He was more, however, than Damon Bailey, the player. He was Damon Bailey, the unassuming kid next door, the son every father would cherish, an inspiration to a generation of young followers.

In eight years, he had played before 2.5 million fans in gymnasiums, hundreds of millions more on television. He had become a legend, perhaps the most recognized—and most popular—figure in Indiana. Governor Evan Bayh concedes as much. Bayh stopped in a restroom before an address at a hotel in Bedford and listened as two men entered without noticing him.

"Hey," one asked the other, excitedly, "wasn't that Damon Bailey out there?" The other said it was, then added, "I hear the governor is here, too."

His partner replied, almost disinterestedly, "Oh." In Indiana politics is a game, basketball is serious business.

♣   ♣   ♣

Fame and adulation have not changed Damon. He remains as unpretentious as he was back on that Saturday in his freshman year in high school when he sat for his first extensive interview.

He had taken the high road to Great Expectations and thousands of fans had been along for the ride. It had been a grand trip, a journey Damon insists is not over.

Join him now as he relives his dream.

—**Wendell Trogdon**

CONTENTS

PART I

An Overview . . . . Page 13

PART II

Dad And Mom . . . . Page 16

PART III

The Early Years . . . . Page 27

PART IV

Damonmania . . . . Page 37

PART V

Sound Advice . . . . Page 47

PART VI

Second Chance . . . . Page 49

PART VII

Frustration Season . . . . Page 59

PART VIII

Road To The Top . . . . Page 69

PART IX

Coach Dan Bush . . . . Page 93

PART X

All-Star Summer . . . . Page 96

Picture Section . . . . Page 97

PART XI

The Freshman . . . . Page 117

PART XII
My Sister Courtney . . . . Page 126

PART XIII
Better Days . . . . Page 131

PART XIV
Peaks And Valleys . . . . Page 136

PART XV
Looking For Damon . . . . Page 140

PART XVI
On To Minneapolis. . . . . Page 143

PART XVII
Staying Put . . . . Page 147

PART XVIII
Conference Title. . . . . Page 150

PART XIX
Last And Best . . . . Page 165

PART XX
The Farewell . . . . Page 174

PART XXI
Coach Bob Knight . . . . Page 179

PART XXII
The Fans . . . . Page 185

PART XXIII
Awaiting The Draft. . . . . Page 192

A Postscript . . . . Page 200

PART I

AN OVERVIEW

We had won the title, beating the best players in America for the 1983 national championship. The most valuable player of that age 11-and-under Amateur Athletic Union tournament at Notre Dame was about to be named.

I had been taught to win, not to seek individual attention. So I had not thought about the MVP award until I heard the tournament director announce:

"And the most valuable player of the tournament, Damon Bailey."

That was a special moment for me, a feeling of accomplishment for a 11-year-old boy from an obscure and tiny Indiana town. I had been around gymnasiums since I was two, had played on teams that won tournaments, had been MVP several times, but those were local events.

This was different. We had faced the finest teams in the nation in our age group, beaten America's best players our age, the elite among a select few. And I was—at least to observers there—the outstanding player among them.

Tom "Red" Taylor, our coach, said later the committee had not bothered to vote for an MVP. The consensus was so obvious, he was told, no ballot was needed after our victories over teams from Virginia and Las Vegas.

It was a heady feeling and I was elated, especially because a broken leg had kept me from playing as a 10-year-old the previous year in the age 11-and-under finals.

I knew, however, not to be too pleased with myself. My parents, Beverly and Wendell, would not tolerate any smugness, would find a way to keep such recognition from expanding the size of my head.

Our local newspaper, the *Bedford Times-Mail*, was not impressed either. When a member of my family submitted a team picture with a story of the team championship and my MVP award, the editors chose not to run it. It was ironic, considering the attention I would get later.

No matter! Standing there with the MVP trophy, I realized for the first time that I might be able to really accomplish something with this game called basketball. That award brought into focus what might be ahead if I continued to work, continued to dedicate myself to perfecting my game, or at least make it as good as I could make it.

As far back as I can remember basketball has been a big part of my life. I cannot recall a thing for me that dates back farther. I am very fortunate that I fell in love with the game at an early age.

The hours learning the game, practicing and playing it, were never work for me. It was something I enjoyed, whether it was in competitive games or practicing alone at home or at the gym a mile away in Heltonville.

My first outside goal was a metal rim on a plywood board nailed to a utility pole in the back yard. I was little, four, maybe five, at the time, and the goal was seven or eight feet high. My "hardwood" was yard grass. That did not matter. It was a place to shoot, to learn the game.

That, however, was not my first encounter with basketball. My introduction to the sport came when I was barely out of diapers and went with my dad to independent games.

He was a student of the game, knew what it took to be a good player. He exposed me to the sport, taught me how it should be played.

If I did not fall asleep in the bleachers at those independent games, I would mess around with the ball on the floor during warmups and at half time.

My first broken bone resulted at one of those games. Dad and the older players were shooting at the Bedford Boys Club and, of course, I also was out on the floor with them. I fell for some reason and one of Dad's teammates accidentally stepped on my arm, breaking it.

I kept on going to my Dad's games as long as he played. I was growing up with him, shooting during timeouts and at half time.

In time I grew to love the game. A lot of people like sports, enjoy playing them. It was deeper than that for me. It was a love affair, an infatuation that did not lose its attraction as I grew older.

Basketball was never a chore to me. It was not work to go out and play. If it was 100 degrees out, chances are I was out practicing. I may have been hot and steamy but I was enjoying it.

The rewards would come later. It is, I am sure, the dream of almost every kid who plays basketball, especially in Indiana, to be considered a hero, to win a state championship, to be Mr. Basketball, to attend a major state university, to be recognized.

Basketball allowed me to live a dream, to do all those things, to be that kind of person. I have been there, done that, been a winner.

There is not a thing in my life I would change other than my sister Courtney's bout with leukemia. That taught me that life is a mixture of good and bad, that not every day is brightened with sunshine.

The recognition I received was a mixture of good and bad. It was a good feeling, knowing that fans appreciated what I had accomplished, that they respected me as a player and as a person. All that attention—the requests for autographs, the demands on my time—robbed me of some of my youth. At times it seemed my high school and college years were lived in a fish bowl under a continual spotlight.

That adoration was fun at times. At times it became a distraction. Chances are, however, I would have missed it had it not been there.

PART II

DAD AND MOM

It is doubtful any parents were more involved in what their son was doing than mine. They made a lot of sacrifices that allowed me to be successful in basketball. Their guidance and moral values helped shape the kind of person I am.

Children cannot choose when they are born or to whom. I could not have arrived at a better time or had better parents. Dad was 21 when I was born, Mom was 20. We sort of grew up together. They were young, able to take part in some of the things I enjoyed doing.

Basketball had always been a part of their lives. Dad had been an outstanding high school player at Heltonville, averaging 15.3 points in a 61-game career from 1966-1968. Those who saw him play rated him among the top five players in the school's history. My mother had been a cheerleader at Tunnelton, another Lawrence County school.

Heltonville, like Tunnelton, is small village America. It might have 500 residents if census takers counted far enough beyond the town limits. The post office does not have enough business to stay open 8 hours a day and the only place to buy a Coke or a sack of groceries is at the store owned by Larry "Bonehead" Faubion. Most social activity centers around the grade school or the Baptist, Methodist and Christian churches.

The stone mill at the edge of town has been out of business for years and most of the men either farm, drive school buses, cut timber or work in Bedford. My Dad, for example, was transportation director for the Bedford North Lawrence school system when I was in high school. Women, like my Mom, work at banks, businesses or other places "in town," which is how we referred to Bedford.

It is there—around Heltonville and Tunnelton—where at least four generations on both sides of my family have lived since before the turn of the century.

Nothing came easy for my ancestors or anyone else who lived in the area. Survival depended on hard work, a trait, like the color of one's eyes, that was passed on from one generation to the next. Success was earned through effort.

The results were men and women with character, solid as the limestone buried in the area's hills, people without pretense. It was into that background that my parents were born.

It was a time when almost every hamlet had a high school and each school had a basketball team which gave residents a sense of identification.

That meant both my parents had been around basketball most of their lives, enjoyed the sport, knew the game. Both were very involved in what I did, but they never criticized any of my coaches, not from grade school through college. If I did not play much in grade school, for example, Mom and Dad did not get mad at the coach as most parents did. Mom usually kept quiet. Dad got upset at me, told me I needed to work harder.

I feel fortunate I had a father who was still active when I was growing up. When I wanted to go out and play basketball, baseball or whatever game it was, he went out and played with me.

He ran with me after he came home from work, showed me the importance of conditioning, made sure I knew what it took to be successful in sports. We ran hundreds of miles together, still do from time to time.

Dad laughs now that it is a good thing I was born first, claiming he might not have had that much energy if I had been the second child born four years later.

We spent countless hours across the road at the baseball diamond at Pleasant Run Park hitting and catching pop ups. I can remember hundreds of times when we played basketball in the paved driveway after I graduated from my backyard goal.

If Dad was not around to retrieve the ball when I shot, Mom or Courtney, when she became old enough, were. I had to ask only once, never twice, and they were out there with me.

I often have been asked to name the greatest coach I have been around. That is a difficult question because I have been around a lot of them and played for a number of them. Dan Bush, my high school coach at Bedford North Lawrence, was a great coach. Coach Knight at Indiana obviously is a great coach. I think, though, that the person I learned the most from, listened to the most, was definitely my Dad.

Dad introduced me to the game. He taught me the game. He showed me how it should be played. When I did not play well, or shoot well in high school and college, he would suggest we practice at the school gym at Heltonville. He always helped me find what was wrong, whether it was my shot, my lack of concentration, or whatever.

If he did not notice I needed to correct a fault in my game, I would ask him to work with me. He would stop whatever he was doing and we would spend an hour or six hours, however long it took to fix what was wrong.

No matter how good a player is, there will be times when technique, shooting form or even the basics of the game need work. We did that, made corrections, in those sessions at the gym.

Dad was very demanding. He saw early on what I could do, knew that if I put forth the effort I could be a special player. Had he not seen that potential he probably would not have been as tough on me as he was.

Everyone needs a kick in the rear now and then and Dad did not hesitate to give me one when I needed it. If he knew, for example, I had planned to run in the morning, he'd get me up and send me on my way, even though I would have preferred to stay in bed for another half hour. It is easier to say at 9 p.m. you are going to run the next morning than it is to get up at 6 a.m. and do it.

I have never regretted the way he went about things. I appreciate it. Some people may have thought he was too hard on me, that he should have done this or he should have done that. I may have thought the same way those critics did when I was eight or nine. Looking back, however, there is nothing he did that was not for my benefit. Whatever he did was to help me be a better person and a better player and for that I will always be grateful.

Dad taught me that the quantity of time spent at practice was not nearly as important as the quality of the effort. If I spent 15 minutes concentrating on the game and 105 minutes goofing around, I was not doing myself any good. Dad never allowed me to do that.

If we were going to practice, we were going to work at something, one-on-one drills, shooting, one or two specific things. We were not going out there to throw up hook shots from the free throw line or jack around.

I was out there to get better and I had people out there trying to help me get better. Otherwise, I was wasting my time, Dad's time, Mom's time and Courtney's time.

A lot of kids today probably spent more time in their driveways than I did. I did, however, play more than most kids my age because I was in a lot of games and on a lot of teams—Boys Club, grade school, AAU—from the time I was six years old.

We never kept a progress chart or listed how many free throws I made or how many shots I hit. The only thing I ever charted was how high I could jump. I kept marks on the wall in the basement so I could see if I could jump higher from one week to the next.

I do not believe charts are as important as working on your game and knowing you are doing it right. There will be some days you can do everything right but your shots will not fall. When that happens you have to keep doing other things—rebound, pass, play solid defense—until the ball starts going in the hole.

Dad made certain I had the right form, used the right release, had my legs straight, that I did not jump sideways when I shot. Habits, he said, were hard to break. "Do something right long enough and you'll forget how to do it wrong," he insisted.

He preached, "Repetition! Repetition! Repetition! Repetition! Elbow in, not out." A lot of kids shoot with their elbows out when they are young in order to get the ball to the basket. Dad would not allow me to do that.

"Get the right technique now and you'll eventually be able to shoot from further out on the floor," he said.

I am right handed, but I learned to shoot a left-handed lay up at an early age. It was not because I was any more gifted, it was because Dad and I spent hours working at it.

I could do that and other things with a basketball when I was eight or nine because I had a father who understood the game and worked with me.

I learned a lot from Dad at a young age. Some kids do not learn these things until they are in high school. We reviewed games from the time I first played at the Boys Club. When we returned home Dad would explain what I did well, what I should have done that I did not do. I listened because I knew he did not want me to make the same mistake twice.

That post-game education may be one of the reasons why a lot of people think I may be smarter basketball-wise than the average player. I think I am, too. I am not an intelligent player because I just played the game, practiced it. It was those critiques by Dad of how I had played, his reminders of what I should have done, that gave me a better understanding of the game.

One example of what my Dad taught me came after a game at the Boys Club. I saved a ball from going out of bounds under the other team's basket, but threw it directly to an opposing player for a layup. When we returned home, Dad explained what I should have done.

"When you save the ball in enemy territory, throw it long," he said. "If your man gets it fine. If the opponent grabs it, he is a long way from his basket and your team has a chance to play defense."

These kinds of instructions continued for a long time but to a lesser degree as I grew up.

Another thing my parents did that helped my game was make it possible for me to compete against players who were older than I was. Opponents who were older, bigger and stronger forced me to do things I would not have been able to do until later. I could not shoot over bigger players, I had to learn to score another way. I could not block their shots, so I had to learn to keep them from getting the ball.

I played against older kids at the Boys Club, competed against sixth graders when I was in the third grade, faced eighth graders when I was in the seventh grade, went up against seniors when I was a freshman.

I learned a lot playing against Dad and some of his friends at the Heltonville gym. Guys like "Bonehead" Faubion may not have been the greatest players in the world, but I was eight or nine going up against 25-year-old men.

They did not give me any breaks, made no concessions, threw me against the wall like they did each other. If I went in for a layup, they tried to block the shot if they had to knock me down to do it. They scraped me off the floor and sent me back down court on defense. They treated me just like they did Dad or anyone else.

That did not bother me. I might have gotten discouraged playing against those guys, but I never quit. Before long I could hold my own with them, then eventually passed them up as I grew up and they grew older.

They made me excel. One night they razzed me about not being able to jump high enough to touch the top of the square over the basket. I said I could, but not for fun. "Put some money up there and I'll show you," I said.

Jerry Hawkins put up a $5 bill. Someone else pulled out another $5 bill. Bruce "Ike" Whitridge, one of the men, crawled over the backboard and held the two bills at the top of the square. They were mine, he said, if I could reach them. I went home $10 richer with another incentive to jump higher.

Because of those experiences I was better at a young age than other kids. It was easier to score against players my age, rebound against kids my size, and do things those who did not have my background could not.

The support of my family, the instructions I was taught by my Dad and the opportunity to play against better, stronger and older opponents were among the most important factors in my success.

As soon as Dad saw how good I could be, he taught me that the true sign of a great player was one who made everyone around him better. I remember one time when I did not throw the ball to a kid on my team who was open. I probably thought he could not catch it and he probably would not have.

I explained that to Dad who said, "Throw it to him anyhow. If he doesn't catch it that's not your fault. You will get to a point where you will be playing with kids who are going to catch it."

I realized then that the kid did not make the catch that day because I had not thrown him the ball. If I had made the pass and he had made the catch for a basket it would have made him a better player, not because of my ability, but because of something I had done. The basket, had he made it, might have inspired his parents to work with him as my Dad had worked with me.

That may be the single most important thing a player can do, not necessarily score 30 points or get 30 rebounds, but make everyone else on the team better.

Dad warned me there would be games when I might not score a lot, that I might be double-teamed or triple-teamed. Some nights, he said, the shots would not fall no matter what, nights when I would not be able to throw the ball in the ocean. On those occasions, he said, I would need to do other things to help my team win.

One game that stands out was against Perry Meridian, an Indianapolis metropolitan area school, when I was a sophomore. I did not shoot well, hit 5 of 14 shots from the field, 8 of 12 from the free throw line, and scored 18 points.

That may have been a good game for some players, but I did not think I had played well. What was significant was that I had done more than score. I pulled down 17 rebounds and had seven assists.

I realized that night what Dad had meant when he said I could do things other than score to help my team win.

I take great pride in the fact that I have been a winner at every level I have played, whether it be at the Boys Club, AAU, grade school, junior high or college. I am proud of that because I have been a big part of it. I have done what it takes to make my team better, whether it was to score points, play defense, rebound or distribute the ball to shooters.

Dad taught me to throw the ball to another player if he was open. "Give up the ball," he kept telling me. I scored a lot of points, but I never shot a lot. I never considered myself a selfish player. Neither did my teammates.

I learned early that I had better never act conceited, be cocky or become a show-off. One incident remains with me as clearly as if it occurred yesterday. Like most mothers, Mom remained quiet when Dad was criticizing me or explaining how things should be done. She and I were in one room after a junior high game and I had acted conceited or, perhaps, boasted about how well I played.

Dad was in another room. I must have said something that caught his attention. He yelled in, "Damon! No one likes a hot dog."

I said, loud enough for him to hear, "I do—with ketchup and mustard." My Mom said, "Oh, my." She knew I was in trouble. Dad stormed into the room. He was unglued. After he straightened me out that night, I never dared act conceited again.

I could write a separate book about the things my Dad and I have done, the things he and my mother have taught me, the sacrifices they have made for me. I cannot express in words the love and feelings I have for them.

They made a lot of sacrifices for me. They drove thousands of miles to take me to my AAU practices and to games those summers I played with Municipal Gardens. It was not easy for them to drive to Brownsburg or Indianapolis. Those were 130-to-140 mile round trips, two or three a week, more in the weeks

Mom and Dad—ready to leave for another game

before a major tournament. We often did not return home until after midnight and Mom and Dad would have to be up at 6 a.m. to go to work.

That was not for a short time, that was for the entire summer. They missed very few games. I think Mom attended every AAU tournament I played, regardless of where it was. Dad could not get away for the start of a national tournament in Seattle, but he flew out later.

Wherever it was, Tampa, Des Moines, Washington, D.C., or Jonesboro, Ark., they were there, or at least one of them was.

That was very unusual, and very important to me. A lot of parents could not or would not make that sacrifice of time and money. Some players were sent with the coach. Their parents were seldom there, which may have been fine for them. My parents were there cheering for me and for my team.

That may not have meant anything; it may not have made me a better player. I do not know. I do know that if I did not play well or if I thought about giving up, they were there for support.

They may not have said anything, but the fact they were present gave me an extra incentive to do it for them, if not for myself.

I always had a great following from both sides of my family. My grandfather, Russell Case, died when I was young and I do not remember him. My grandmother Case and Grandma and Papaw Bailey (Louise and Jesse) were almost always at my games. So were a lot of my aunts and uncles, 10 to 20 all together.

Tournament and game directors looked forward to my games and not necessarily because I was playing. They often joked that they could count on $200 or $300 extra revenue, just from my family.

That involvement was always important to me, is even today. I did not overlook that support and I never took it for granted. No matter how great you want to do, how much you want to accomplish, there will be times in your life you may feel like quitting. If your Mom and Dad are there, your grandparents are there, your aunts and uncles are there—people who have supported you, made sacrifices for you—you think again. They help give you an extra drive inside. Sure, you are doing it for yourself, but you also are doing it for a lot of people who want to see you do well.

As I have said, Mom and Dad taught me a lot, especially about basketball. They also are responsible for me being the kind of person I am. They did not always tell me what I should do or how I should act. I naturally observed how they acted, how they responded to situations, how they treated other people. I could not have had finer role models.

They did tell me, "Be your own person. Do what you want to do within the parameters we have set. You know what is right and wrong. We know you will do what is right." That freedom may have given me confidence some other kids may not have felt.

They also taught me that I would never be able to please everybody, that I should not be concerned about what others think. I was told to be myself, not to emulate someone else, to be successful in my own way as long as it was within the guidelines they had given me.

They expected a lot of me. They never have been awed by the success I have had with basketball or the honors that have come with it. That is one reason neither they, nor I, were caught up with all the attention, all the press, the radio and television coverage. The accolades were nice, but that was not what I was about. I wanted to be the best player I could be, to be a winner, to help my team win.

Dad never told me I played a great game until the state tournament. Oh, there may have been one or two occasions when he hinted that he knew I was good. He knew what my goals were and he did not want to detract from those objectives.

When I conduct basketball camps today I relate some of the suggestions my Dad gave me. "If you are going to do something, do it right and do it a lot. It takes a lot of sweat, a lot of hours, a lot of work, to be successful. Everyone wants to be great. Few will put in the time it takes to be a winner."

There is no way I can express in words my gratitude for what my parents have done for me. I have tried to repay them by being the son they wanted me to be.

PART III

THE EARLY YEARS

My first involvement in basketball as a team sport came at the Boys Club in Bedford. That, too, was something I was involved in earlier than most kids.

Dick Browning, a friend of my Dad, had a son who played in a seven-year-old league. I was four or five, too young to compete, but Browning let me practice with his team one entire winter. A year later Browning and my Dad obtained a waiver so I could play in games as a six-year old.

I did not care whether players were two years older or 20 years older, I wanted to compete.

Our teams won at the Boys Club and I was in several all-star games. It was there I won my first championships and my first MVP award. Some of my coaches, in addition to Browning, were Pat O'Brien, Jim Allen, Jim Price and Pat Goodin.

A lot of things other kids learned there I already had been taught by my Dad. I was ahead of most of my age group through junior high because of that. I was bigger than other kids my age and the fact I understood the game gave me an extra advantage.

* * *

When I was a second grader at Heltonville, Mark Turner, a teacher and coach, saw me out on the playground with his fifth and sixth graders. He must have been impressed for he kept watch on how I was doing. When I entered the third grade he obtained permission for me to play from Cam Anderson, the principal, and my parents.

Again I would be playing with and against bigger and older players, fifth and sixth graders.

I am sure there was some resentment among some of them, especially those I may have cost some playing time. And I know that a few parents were unhappy, perhaps jealous, because I was playing and their sons were not. I like to think it was minimal because at Heltonville, and elsewhere, I played with good people who had good parents.

I never acted there, or anywhere else, like I was the greatest person who ever played or was ever going to play the game. I loved the game. I got the ball to older students. I did not hog it or shoot every time I had it. I think that really helped to eliminate, as much as possible, the resentment, the jealously that was there.

I approached it as, "Hey I'm not better than you are. Let's make this a special team, the best we can make it." Every team I've played on, every game I've played in, I wanted to play well. There was no doubt about that. But the most important thing was for my team to win and for me to have a part in that whether it called for me to score 30 points or to get the ball to someone else.

We did not lose often, one game when I was in the third grade, one when I was in the fourth. After that I did not play in a losing game, not even in AAU ball, until I was a freshman in high school.

I do not remember much about any specific game in grade school. I do recall we played Parkview, a Bedford school that had been considered the best grade school team in the county for several years. I was really excited, knowing the caliber of the competition. We won that game, 39-24, then beat Parkview again the next year, 47-32.

Shawswick had good teams, too. One of the players there was Dwayne Curry, who would become my teammate on our championship team at Bedford North Lawrence High School.

I want to pay tribute to the late Mr. Turner, who was my coach at Heltonville. We had a unique relationship. He thought a lot of me and I did of him, even at that young age. He was very important in my life, letting me play with the older kids. That may not be unusual today, but when I was in school it was rare then for a third grader to compete against sixth graders. It gave me an opportunity to be better. I feel what I learned by playing in the third and fourth grades was beneficial to me later.

Turner knew I was very competitive, that I did not like to lose. He knew I loved to be challenged. He would sometimes bet me a Coke that I would not score 100 on a math test. He would set goals for me, then wager that I could not meet them. He told adults later that I almost lived on the Cokes he had to buy to pay off his bets. None of those challenges, I might add, involved basketball.

I did not always get 100 on those math tests or win all the bets, but I tried. If someone tells me I cannot do something, I will try to prove him wrong.

As I have said, I love playing basketball. I love the game. If the game was not competitive, however, I'm not sure I would care for it as much. I am competitive regardless of the challenge. If it is basketball, that is what I'm going to be successful at. If it's a business, I'm going to make it a success. If I decide to be a lawyer, I'll be the best lawyer in town because I know what it takes to be successful.

I'm not the smartest person who ever lived, never claimed to be, but I do know to be successful you have to be dedicated, have great desire and have confidence in yourself.

If I'm going to do something, I'm going to set high goals. If I do not reach all of them I will not have cheated myself. I feel there is no point in doing something if you do not give it all you have.

* * *

My initiation into Amateur Athletic Union basketball came through my affiliation with a Bedford Boys Club all-star team when I was nine.

We were in a tournament at Rhodius Park in Indianapolis and had played Garfield Park several times. Kevin Newbold, a very good player on that Garfield team, was already playing AAU ball with Municipal Gardens.

Kevin's dad had told "Red" Taylor, the Municipal Gardens coach, about me. I had never heard of Tom "Red" Taylor, or Municipal Gardens or the Amateur Athletic Union. AAU basketball was not as big then as it is today, especially as far as the number of teams that compete. Back then only the good players played; the others did not.

Taylor came to watch me play in that tournament. After the game he invited me to try out for his nine-year-old team, although he would say later he already knew he wanted me as a player.

I was against joining Municipal Gardens at the time, thinking it might be difficult playing with kids I did not know and for a coach I had just met.

I should explain that, even today, I am a relatively shy person. So at that time I was not eager for that new experience.

Dad, once again, gave me a figurative kick in the butt and a look that said, "Oh, yes, you will." He explained that I would be playing with some of the best players in the state and against some of the most talented kids in the country.

I consented for even at that young age I knew my parents would not lead me astray. We went up for the tryout, I made the team as "Red" already knew I would and we went on to win five national championships and I was the MVP in four of those tournaments.

It was a great experience. Taylor, who continued to coach our teams all those years, was another person who was very influential in how I played the game. He demanded, "Give it up. Be unselfish. Go all out. Play as hard as you can."

It was unbelievable how well our AAU teams played together. To have the caliber of players we had and to have the cohesion, the unselfishness, the bond we formed was amazing. We did not always have the best teams, but we had players who did certain parts of the game well. If they had a role, they performed it, did not try to do more than they were capable of doing.

At one time, we had a 73 and 1 tournament record against the best players in America our age.

"Red" was a great coach. Everyone who is involved in AAU basketball at the national level knows "Red" Taylor because of the national championships his teams have won.

Among the players on those various AAU teams were Matt Waddell, Tipton, and Linc Darner, Anderson Highland, both of whom played at Purdue; twins Jon and Joe Ross, Northfield, who played at Notre Dame; Steve Mozingo, Franklin Central, who went to Taylor; Elliott Hatcher, Ritter, who played in California; Troy Terrill, Lebanon, Indiana-Purdue University, Indianapolis; Kyle Kenworthy, Brebeuf High School, and Lloyd Carr, Pike High School.

We were joined later by Eric Montross, the 7-0 center who led Lawrence North to the state high school championship in 1989 and was on the 1993 North Carolina NCAA title team. Alan Henderson, who later played with me at Indiana, was on our last AAU team.

Our edge came in the chemistry we developed, a togetherness that was unusual for players that young. It showed the importance of cooperation and unselfishness, the necessity for role players, the need to sacrifice one's desires and ambitions for the good of a team.

Those AAU teams were proof that the five best players may not make the best team. Basketball is not a game of five stars. Good teams can have players with limited ability and talent. I consider myself one of those people. I am not 7 feet tall or extremely quick or the best athlete around. I can run, I can jump, I can pass and I can score, but I do not consider myself a great athlete. Players with limited abilities need to learn to do something special, something extra, at each level as they progress.

* * *

Like most students, I may have had some apprehension when I moved from Heltonville Elementary to Shawswick Junior High. I would have a new basketball coach, Carl Cox, and new teachers. And it was a much bigger school, one of three junior highs that feed into Bedford North Lawrence High School.

I need not have been concerned. Junior High turned out to be a fun time in my life. I started meeting people other than those I had known at Heltonville for six years.

Cross country, I found, was a good conditioner for basketball. I ran on the junior high team, usually winning most local meets. After I set a few course records, the coaches started holding me back, making me wait 30 seconds to a minute after the other runners had started, thinking I might be better tested if I had a handicap. I still usually won because the delayed starts did not count against me.

In invitational events elsewhere, I did well, winning a couple of events, usually finishing in the top five. Just being a runner was not good enough for me. If I was going to run I wanted to be the best runner on the team. I went to all the practices and often ran again when I returned home. Second best was not good enough if I could possibly do better.

* * *

I had fun playing basketball at Shawswick. That was when all the recognition started. Fans began to notice me, to know who I was, when I went to Bedford. I had my first request for an autograph when I was in the eighth grade. Junior high would be a turning point in my life.

If I ever had a hint of being cocky or having a big head I think that was the time. That did not happen. My parents saw to that. They could always put the situation into perspective.

Once again I was playing with students older than I, a seventh grader on an eighth-grade team. That was rare because the school also had a seventh grade team. I am not sure I was the first one, but I was the only seventh grader to play on the older team that year.

The eighth graders, who had won just two games the previous season, accepted me even though I may have taken a spot occupied by one of their classmates. It helped for me to have played at Heltonville with Jimmy Jones and Barry Staggs, who were starters for Shawswick. It was not like I was coming in, did not know the kids or had not played with and against some of them in the past.

We won our first game and continued to win. I am not sure how many people attended the first few games, but the crowds grew each time we played.

I do not recall many specifics about any of the games until we faced Bedford. Its fans were certain our streak was about to end. So were some of our own fans. We were the Shawswick Farmers, country kids who would be no match for the team from the city. Or so they said.

On that Bedford Stonecutters team were Brent Byrer, Derek Clouse and Eric Flynn, who would be my teammates in high school. We beat Bedford, despite that talent, and fans became more interested in what we were doing out there at Shawswick.

I remember playing Oolitic in a tournament at the end of the season. We had to go into overtime, maybe it was double overtime, to beat them and remain unbeaten.

By the time the season was over we were drawing 400 to 500 fans a game.

As a seventh grader I could dunk anything I could palm, a tennis ball or a golf ball for example. Over the following summer I learned to palm the basketball and in a short time I could dunk it, too.

It was the year, I believe, that I received my first letter from a college coach. We were in a physical education class when Coach Cox handed me a letter from Jim Boeheim, the Syracuse coach, who asked:

"How would you like to play before 41,000 fans in the Carrier Dome?"

I stuffed the letter in my gym trunks. I did not even tell my parents about it until Cox asked Dad if I had mentioned it. I probably knew my Dad and Mom wanted me to be a kid, to live for today, not be concerned about five years down the road.

* * *

I continued to play with Coach Taylor's AAU team that summer.

Our team won the national 13-and-under tournament in 1985 at Carver-Hawkeye Arena at the University of Iowa, defeating New Orleans, 48-47.

Coach Taylor recalls that New Orleans went ahead 47-46 with 20 seconds remaining in the game. He called a timeout, set up a play in which I inbounded the ball, then stepped back onto the court for a pass. My teammates cleared out one side of the floor, allowing me to drive the length of the court for a basket.

That may have been the first time I was quoted in a news story. I do not remember the interview, but according to the Associated Press, I said something like, "Coach Taylor told me to take it to the hole and that's what I did."

Again I was fortunate to win the tournament MVP award.

* * *

When basketball season started at Shawswick that fall, I was with players my own age. One of them was Dwayne Curry, who I knew from playing against in grade school, and Jay Faubion, who had been with me at Heltonville.

Fans expected a lot. After a few victories, all 1,500 seats were filled and fans lined the walls for each home game.

By then I was getting some mention in the *Bedford Times-Mail*, but I am not sure I always read it.

A few games that year stand out in my memory. I remember the Bedford game for two reasons.

One of the Bedford cheerleaders was Stacey Ikerd, the girl I would marry after dating nine years. That was the first, or one of the first times, I met her, and we talked later. I have never let her forget who won that game.

The other reason is because of something my Dad said. I had been out of school for three or four days with mononucleosis and I did not want to play, really did not feel that well. Dad, however, reminded me that I would, like everyone else, have to do things in life I did not always want to do. "Life is not easy," he said. "You have to play sick at times. You will have to go to work at times when you are sick."

He looked at me and asked, "If Dr. J. were sick today, do you think he wouldn't play?" I knew the answer he expected. I went to class a half day before the game so I could play, then missed another day or two afterward.

I hit a half-court shot coming across the 10 second line as the clock ended a quarter. We won by a bunch and I probably left the floor hoping that Stacey would be impressed.

We did not have many close games that season. Unlike the previous season, we rolled over Oolitic, 57-17, in a game in which I scored 31 points. I liked to score, of course, but I liked getting my teammates involved, too. I was, by then, being guarded at times by two players. When that happened it was fun to flip a pass to an open player for an easy score.

* * *

That was the year Bob Knight came to two of our games, which I believe was after I scored 46 points when we defeated Seymour, 53-42. I did not know until after the first game that he was there.

I may have wondered why Coach Cox left me in so long in the game against Eastern Green. He always removed the starters when we were beating a team easily, never liked to run up scores. That night he let me play almost the entire game, explaining later that Knight had not driven to Shawswick from Bloomington just to see me play two quarters.

Cox later apologized for running up the score to Joe Sichting, the Eastern coach and brother of Jerry Sichting, the former NBA player from Martinsville.

I did know Coach Knight was in the crowd when he returned for a second game. Some time later, Knight's comments about me being a better guard than anyone on the I.U. team were printed. The statement appeared later in John Feinstein's national best seller, *A Season on the Brink.*

Those comments were nice. I did not, however, take them seriously. Even as an eighth grader I knew that if, and when, I played for Knight I would have to prove what I could do, not use a press clipping from my eighth grade year to impress him.

Chances are I was more concerned at the time about another coach who was at our games more often than Bob Knight. That coach was Dan Bush for whom I would play at Bedford within a few months.

*　*　*

I am sometimes asked if the crowds made me nervous at that young age. I do not think I ever have been nervous before a game. At times I was excited but I never had that butterfly feeling as far as playing a game. There were times that I could not wait for a game. It never bothered me, though, whether I was playing in front of 10 fans or 40,000. I never noticed the crowd once the game started.

One reason I may not have been nervous was because I always had confidence in myself and in my team. I never have entered a game that I did not feel I was going to play well or that my team would not win. I did not always play well and my team did not always win, but it was not because I did not think we could.

PART IV

DAMONMANIA

That summer of 1986 was one I will not forget. It was an event-filled three months and I did not have a lot of time to ponder my move up from Shawswick Junior High to Bedford North Lawrence High School.

Once again our AAU team won the national title at Orlando, defeating a team from Washington, D.C., 82-64.

I did not know it at the time, but an observer for Coach Knight was there. Coach Taylor recalls that after a preliminary game in which I scored 53 points, the scout said he was convinced and returned to Indiana.

Again I was happier with the championship than with the MVP award.

It also was the summer I flew to New York City to have my picture taken for a *Sports Illustrated* story which rated me as the best incoming high school freshman in the nation.

It was a good experience, but I remember thinking that Heltonville never looked so good when I returned from that metroplex on the Hudson River.

All that attention was a reward, I suppose, for the hard work and practice I had put into the game most of my young life. Rather than bask in the limelight, I used that recognition as an incentive to continue to improve my game. If I was the best freshman in the country I would have to prove it.

Fans already had great expectations for Bedford North Lawrence, some forecasting four straight trips to the State Finals, an accomplishment few, if any, teams ever achieve.

I had not yet played a high school game, had not proved I could play at that level, but I had no doubt that I could.

* * *

At Bedford North Lawrence I started associating with some of the older players, became a part of their group. I was hanging around with seniors, or seniors were hanging around with a freshman, whichever way you want to look at it.

I accompanied Rusty Garrison and Ernie Lovell and our dates to football homecoming that fall. That association helped us get to know each other better. It was a good relationship, considering I was a freshman and they were upperclassmen.

Troy Ikerd, another of the players, was from Heltonville so I had known him for years.

I remember vividly that first practice at BNL. Coach Bush called us together, looked around at each player, and said, "Like it or not this sophomore (pointing to Brent Byrer) and this freshman (meaning me) are going to be a big part of this team. If anyone can't accept that, the door is over there. You can leave now."

Chances are, the coach knew the character of his players. None departed.

It was almost a given from that first day that I would play a lot. That made me work even harder, I think. Coach Bush had gone out on the limb by putting that much faith in me and responsibility on me. If he was going to stick his neck out for me, I would have to play well. We were in this together and I did not want to let him down.

Practice went well. The question around Heltonville, Bedford and other towns that make up the school system was whether I would start.

Coach Bush tried to lower any expectations fans might have. "He's ready," he told the *Bedford Times-Mail*, but added, "People should realize this is a big step for him."

I really appreciated another comment he made at that time and would make often in the next four years. "Damon," he said, "is the kind of player who could never score a point and still help his team." It was good to know that the coach considered me a complete ball player.

For a player, the time before that first game of the season passes slowly. That wait for November 22 seemed as long as the anticipation of Christmas had been when I was young. I was not yet old enough to drive, only a month into my fifteenth year, and I was about to compete in one of the toughest basketball conferences in Indiana.

I knew before the opener that I would start the game, but I was not sure what to expect. I had associated with the upperclassmen, had practiced with them. I still wondered what would happen when fans filled the stands, the spotlight came on and the game started. Players sometimes do things in games they have not done in practice.

I need not have been concerned. I took only six shots, five of which were good, not because someone failed to get me the ball. Scottsburg played a zone and, as an inside player, I did not have that many opportunities to shoot. I ended the game with 20 points, hitting 10 of 12 free throws, four rebounds and two assists. More importantly, however, was the fact we won, 82-70.

That game answered a lot of questions in the older players' minds. It helped convince them that I could play against the same competition they could.

I remember telling Bob Bridge, sports editor of the *Times-Mail*, "This is fun. I can't believe how good Lovell and Garrison are." Bridge may have felt I was trying to deflect attention from myself, but I was serious. My respect for them and my teammates would continue to grow.

We followed the Scottsburg game with victories over Salem, a game in which I dunked a shot for the first time in high school, and Bloomington North.

I had not played in a losing game since I was in the fourth grade at Heltonville.

That would change. We traveled to Indianapolis and lost to Cathedral, 44-41. My 23 points did not offset the disappointment of defeat. It would be the first of only 11 losses over a four-year high school career, 11 defeats I would remember much longer than 99 victories.

I had 10 rebounds against Edgewood the next game, but hit only 4 of 12 shots from the field and finished with 13 points in a 52-46 victory. As Dad had warned me, it was a night the shots did not fall, but I helped the team with those 10 rebounds and four assists.

Our ancient rival, Bloomington South, was next on the schedule. I remember I was pumped up all day for the game. I could not wait to play. I do not know whether it was because I had played against Chris Lawson in the past, or because South was considered one of the premiere teams in the state. Perhaps it was because I thought I had played poorly against Edgewood. Whatever the reason, I remember sitting at school, eager, mad at the world all day, just wanting to play.

The junior varsity game went into overtime and that delay made me even more anxious. It just seemed to take forever for the varsity game to begin. The South gym was packed, the crowd mostly BNL fans who irritated the Bloomington South players with boasts that we would win.

As the teams greeted each other before the tip, a South player started talking trash to me, razzing me about being a freshman who was out of his league. I had never ever talked trash or taunted a player. It is not something that is a part of what I am. I looked at him and said, "Hang on for the ride."

Rusty Garrison, who was 6-3, got the tip against Lawson, who was 6-10. I got the ball, drove around a South defender and missed a layup. I guess I was too pumped up. Chances are my tormentor thought he had me spooked.

Once the adrenaline stopped pumping, I hit 15 of my next 17 shots, added seven free throws and finished with 37 points. That was secondary. We won, 73-62.

It was by far my best game to that point and I guess you could say it was the game when I arrived as a high school player. The media in the area started getting even more interested because we had beaten a top-rated team with players who not only were big but good. I really do not know when I started getting attention in the state press. We did not take any state papers, just the *Bedford Times-Mail* and I probably did not read it every night.

I continued to play well after that game. It was the second victory in a 10-game winning streak in which I averaged 25.5 points a game.

One of those victories was over an outstanding Jennings County team. We won that game, 58-48, then defeated the Panthers again in the Seymour sectional. Those were the only games Jennings County lost all season.

The last victory in that winning streak was against Jeffersonville on the road. It was an offensive pell-mell marathon, both teams running up and down the court for 32 minutes. We won, 103-92, and I scored 40, which was the school record at the time.

Our pleasure with that conference victory was short-lived. We lost to Terre Haute South, 74-63, the next night. The first shot I took was an air ball. Everyone on our team played horribly. The scorebook showed I scored 29 points, but there is little consolation in a loss.

The *Louisville Courier-Journal* had covered the Jeffersonville game and fans at Floyd Central, which is in that area, anticipated our game there a week later. We defeated the Highlanders, 68-53, before a packed house in a gym that was extremely hot.

Coach Bush remembers taking me out at one point for a rest. After I went back into the game, he recalls, a woman tapped him on the back until he asked what she wanted.

She then asked, "May I have that cup Damon Bailey used for a drink?"

It was the beginning of "Damonmania" as *The Indianapolis News* labeled it later that season. It also was about the time fans started referring to Heltonville as "Baileysburg."

We lost once more before the regular season ended, falling to Vincennes, 50-48, a game in which I hit only three of nine shots and scored in double figures only because I converted 8 of 10 free throws.

We finished with victories over Martinsville, Evansville Central and Columbus East, three games in which I averaged 28 points. I was happier, though, with the 14 rebounds I had in the game against Columbus East.

* * *

This may be a good time to review the year. Looking back, I think that freshman year was my toughest in high school. I am sure there was a touch of jealousy and I do not think we could have gotten around it. There were seniors sitting on the bench who would have been playing if I was not on the team. I do think, however, everyone—Coach Bush, the players and I—handled it very well.

I would be remiss, too, if I did not say something about Ernie Lovell. Ernie was a very good player and I probably had more fun playing with him than anyone with whom I have ever played. Ernie played the game a lot like I did. He was unselfish. He could shoot, he could score, he could pass, he could do everything. If you were open, Ernie could get you the ball.

That is not to say I did not also enjoy playing with Jay Ritter, Greg Pittman, Brent Byrer, Rusty Garrison and the reserves. Together we had been molded into a team that stood 17-3 going into the tournament.

The Seymour sectional, one of the toughest in the state, was ahead. We drew a bye and faced a good Seymour team, winning 63-60. That set up the championship game against that strong Jennings County team and Coach Joe Null's defensive strategy.

Null's teams were tough for me to play against and that night would be no exception. He used a variety of zone defenses that limited me to six shots and 12 points. What was important, however, was that I was able to dish out six assists. We won, 61-55, and were en route to the regional.

Jay Ritter scored 21 points and three other starters were in double figures, which should have shown critics that we were not a one-man team.

The regional, which also was at Seymour, was not as difficult as the sectional. We played two perennial southern Indiana powers, New Albany and Jeffersonville, defeating both for the second time that season.

Free throws are an important part of basketball and it was never more evident in that 89-64 rout of Jeffersonville. Our team hit 41 of 52 attempts in that game.

I scored 60 points in those two games, but as important to me were my 19 rebounds and 13 assists.

Some critics still insisted we were a one-man team, dependent on me to score. We had proved them wrong before and we did it again in the Evansville semistate. I had trouble with my shot, hitting just 6 of 17 shots and scoring 17 points in the afternoon game against North Harrison. It was another of those games Dad said I could expect. I did help the team with 10 rebounds and six assists. But Jay Ritter, a good shooter, led us to a 70-53 victory with 18 points.

If we were to reach the Final Four we would have to defeat an outstanding Evansville Memorial team that night.

It may have been an omen of good things to come when I went up over 6-8 Cameron Forbes for a layup on one of the first plays of the game. I shot much better—12 of 22 from the field—for 32 points and we defeated Memorial, 59-51, that night.

It was the first semistate title for Bedford-North Lawrence, a 1974 consolidation of Bedford, Fayetteville, Heltonville, Needmore, Oolitic, Shawswick, Tunnelton and part of Williams.

We were on our way to the state finals at Market Square Arena in Indianapolis to face a vaunted Marion team seeking its third straight championship behind the scoring of Jay Edwards and Lyndon Jones.

School was out for spring break that week, but it was practice as usual for the team. The days were filled with hoopla and attention from the media which billed the game as Experience versus Youth. Coach Bush did not let us get caught up with the excitement that surrounded the event to come.

Some fans may have thought a 15-year-old freshman would be nervous playing the defending champions in a 17,000-seat arena. I was not. I do not know if that was because I had played against people like Anfernee Hardaway, Rodney Rogers and

Shawn Bradley in AAU ball or the fact I had competed against so many good players for so long in fieldhouses across the nation.

We played well, trailing Marion 32-30 at the half. I was called for my fourth foul and sat out part of the third quarter. The other players offset my absence and we were behind only 47-46 going into the final period.

I do not remember how much time was left in the game when I fouled out. Anyhow, Marion went on to win, 70-61. That hurt because we had a chance to defeat a team some experts said would rout us from the arena.

Looking back, nine years later, I do not think I played very well in that game. I did score 20 points and snare seven rebounds, but, in hindsight, we might have won had I not been a freshman. It was a situation where I was a rookie playing against Edwards, Jones and other seniors who would go on to win another title.

That feeling remains despite the fact five Marion starters— Edwards, Jones, Daric Keys, Kyle Persinger and Eric Ewer— were named to the Indiana all-star team that year, the only time that has happened.

Some of our fans were irate about some of the fouls called against me in that game. I have never been one to really complain about referees. They have a difficult job. The action is fast, they have 10 players to watch, and they cannot always be in a position to make perfect calls.

I am not going to say I committed all five fouls I was called for in that game. But, yeah, I committed five fouls sometime throughout the game. I probably got by with two or three that were not called. Almost everyone who plays hard is going to commit five fouls, whether they are called or not. He—or she—is going to get called for some that were not committed, but get by with others that were not called.

* * *

My freshman year was over. I shot .497 from the field and scored 637 points for a 23.5 average, and had 227 rebounds and 103 assists. The team finished the season 23-4 and I was named on most all-state first teams. It was a nice honor, but I would have traded it for a state championship for the team.

Still it was a good year as far as any expectations that I, or my family, had. I never imagined I would average that many points or do as well as I had done. Dad and I had talked before the season and we agreed that I should not expect to average more than 10 points a game. We knew I would be facing bigger and older players in bigger gyms where the competition would be more intense.

I was happy with how I had played. And I was grateful the team had been a family, that the players had become my friends. They had made it easier for me.

* * *

That spring I played baseball on the BNL varsity, seeing action as a reserve and pinch runner. I continued to play in the summer league, but gave up the sport because I was involved in AAU basketball. I was missing some practices, a game now and then, and I did not think it was fair to the other players to be a part-time participant.

At that point I decided that I needed to dedicate my time to basketball if I wanted to continue to play at a higher level. I would not have time for baseball and cross country.

I did enjoy baseball, but I knew if I ever was going to make any money in sports it would be in basketball. Had I continued to play baseball and given as much time to it as I did basketball, I might have earned a scholarship in the sport, probably not at Miami or Florida State, but some other college that was not considered a baseball power.

About the only football I played was with neighborhood friends. Mom and Dad steered me away from the game so I never fell in love with the sport, maybe because I never played it competitively.

Softball was for fun. I could relax when I played. We did not practice, just showed up, put on a uniform, ran out on the field and were ready to compete. That does not mean I did not take the game seriously. I have crashed into fences, dived for balls, slid into second base. I want to win regardless of what sport it is.

It is the same way with golf. I like to win, but I took up the game too late to be really good at it. My sole purpose is to be good enough to play with anyone and not be embarrassed with how I play. I play for relaxation. I never expect to shoot par, but I do want to be competitive. That does not mean I rant and rave like some golfers when I do not play well.

I also like to fish and hunt, especially squirrels in the woods around Heltonville. Those are sports that allow me to be alone with my thoughts, isolated from the attention basketball has brought me.

PART V

SOUND ADVICE

It is always beneficial to learn from the experiences of others.

When I was a high school freshman, Steve Alford was an all-American at Indiana and would lead the Hoosiers to their fifth NCAA championship that season.

It was that year I met Alford after an I.U. game at Bloomington. He took Mom, Dad and me out to dinner at the Big Wheel, which is now a Steak N Shake.

As most basketball fans remember, Steve entered I.U. after a highly successful career at New Castle, where his dad, Sam, was coach. He was by then one of the most popular of all the high school stars who had played the game in Indiana.

His name was a household word, his face familiar to basketball fans across the state. He had learned how to cope with attention, face the media, be the object of adulation from fans in this basketball-crazy state.

I had a lot of respect for Steve, both as a person and as a player. I was delighted he had invited us to join him, although it was not an official visit on our part and he made no effort to recruit me as an I.U. player. He did not boast that Indiana was a great place or suggest that I should play there.

As we dined that evening, he reviewed his experiences, told me what to expect, shared how he had handled different situations. He explained what was ahead for me and what I could expect.

He gave us suggestions on how to handle the press and the attention I would be getting in high school. He advised me to keep working hard, not to get a big head, not to forget what had brought me to the position I was in. He mentioned little things we could do, like having an unlisted number at home, staying out of the limelight, avoid letting the attention overtake my love of the game.

Steve knew that every kid wants to see his name in the newspaper, but he said those things could be distracting if I made too much of them. He also said that once I was certain which college I preferred I should make the choice early. "Don't rush into it, but once you are positive, make the decision. You will be amazed at how much pressure that will take off you."

That session with Alford would be very important. It would help me prepare for the attention that was building. I would be grateful in the years to come that he was kind enough to share his insights with us.

PART VI

SECOND CHANCE

That summer of 1987, our 15-and-under AAU team coached by Tom "Red" Taylor won the national championship at Seattle, defeating a Charlotte, N.C. team, 72-62. That brought my fourth MVP trophy.

By then, I had played in so many winning games I began to remember the losses more than the victories. Once we had triumphed, I did not think about it much. I had done what I had to do to help our team win.

When we did lose, I wondered why, pondered what I could have done to help us win. I wanted to make sure that anything I had done wrong would not cost us another victory. If we won, I started thinking about the next game.

That is why I sometimes have to refer to scorebooks and game reports to remember some details.

* * *

Once again Bedford North Lawrence fans anticipated a banner year, their expectations reaching to Indianapolis and another trip to the State Finals at Market Square Arena.

We had lost Ernie Lovell, Rusty Garrison and Eric Hughes, a top reserve, from the previous year. Greg Pittman took over Ernie's spot and Jeff Speer moved into Garrison's center position, joining me, Brent Byrer and Jay Ritter. Brad Noel, Troy Ikerd and Troy Boshears were among the reserves.

I was no longer a freshman. Byrer, Ritter and Pittman had played in the State Finals the year before, which added to the anticipation of the rabid fans waiting to pack each of the 6,300 seats in the BNL gym for every home game.

The state's sports writers ranked us seventh in pre-season polls. The spotlight was on BNL, the team, and Damon Bailey, the player.

We opened the season with a 68-60 victory over Scottsburg, a game in which I scored 28 points and had nine rebounds.

We went on the road to defeat Salem, 80-63, in a game in which I took 24 shots, the most attempts ever for me to that point. I scored 37 and had 10 rebounds, but I was much happier for Coach Bush. It was his 100th victory as mentor of the Stars.

It was obvious in practice that we had good shooters in Pittman and Ritter so I was not too worried about double-team or zone defenses.

When we faced a 2-3 zone against Bloomington North, Pittman zeroed in on all five three-point attempts. That defense did not last long and I ended the game with 30 points on 15 field goals in 22 attempts. BNL won, 81-59.

We looked forward to the Cathedral game, not only because the Irish had beaten us the previous year, ending my personal four-year perfect record, but because they had Sean Wood, an outstanding player who was headed for Kentucky.

We avenged that loss, defeating previously unbeaten Cathedral, 82-76. My 38 points gave me a four-game average of 33.2, a pace I knew I could not maintain over the entire season.

We continued to win, defeating Edgewood, 78-51, and Bloomington South, 66-54, before heading south to New Albany for a Hoosier Hills conference game.

I was not sure what to expect when I missed my first three shots. Things, however, changed quickly. Suddenly I was in a zone and every shot started falling. As an athlete there are times when you can do no wrong. Every shot you take goes in and everything you do is right. This was one of those nights.

I hit 18 straight shots from the field, but I should add this is somewhat deceiving. Some of those shots were layups, some from close in. I finished with 43 points, mainly because my teammates passed the ball to me in a position where I could score.

It was a special moment. I was entrenched in battle—wanting to win—so competitive, so focused, I did not notice a single person was in the gym. Being in a zone is a special occasion for a player.

We won the game, 70-65, and started our pursuit of another conference title.

Those zones, like the one I was in at New Albany, do not last forever. Mine ended the next game against Perry Meridian, which I mentioned earlier. I hit but 5 of 14 shots for 18 points. I did snag 17 rebounds and had seven assists to offset my poor shooting. More importantly, we won the game, 75-51.

Before the holidays we defeated the Cubs at Madison, 59-49. We were 9-0 and I had averaged 31.3 points per game.

* * *

By that time, we were getting more and more attention. The requests for interviews increased. So did phone calls to our home, becoming so numerous we asked for an unlisted number. Coach Bush was getting calls from recruiters and more questions from newsmen.

It was becoming difficult to go to the mall in Bedford or eat out without being asked for autographs or questioned about basketball. About the only place I could be in public and be a part of the crowd was in Heltonville. The people there had known me all my life, did not treat me any different than they did anyone else.

A few strangers were able to find our house even though not many people in Heltonville would give them directions. Missy Allen Perry was sitting with Courtney one night when two girls from out of the area, came into the yard, pulled out some grass, sealed it in plastic bags and drove away.

I was old enough to drive by then so I visited with Stacey, the cheerleader I had met as an eighth grader, on the few Saturday nights when we did not have a game. We did not go out in Bedford often, but sometimes visited friends to avoid attention.

Dad and his friends almost always played basketball in the gym at Heltonville on Sunday nights and I usually was there with them.

* * *

Coach Bush did not give us much time off for Christmas. The toughest part of our season was ahead, 11 games in five weeks against some strong teams.

Our first foe after the break was Jennings County, a game in which I knew I would be closely guarded as I was each time we met the Panthers. I was free for only nine shots, the fewest of the season and ended up with 12 points, my lowest output all year. We won, 65-43, so I was not disappointed.

Terre Haute South was next on our schedule and once again we had an opportunity to avenge a loss from the previous year. South was a tough team, made more so by Tony McGee, a bruising 6-5 all-state football and basketball player, who later would join the Cincinnati Bengals.

Neither team conceded a point. It was a battle from the opening whistle and no one could gain an edge. The game went into overtime. We were still tied with time running out in the overtime when I fired a shot from about the hash mark. I was exhausted, then elated as the shot tickled the nets for a 77-74 victory. That basket gave me 42 points for the night.

I did not know exactly how much time was left in the game until I heard someone yell for me to shoot. I'm not sure whether it was Jay Ritter's dad, Danny, or his grandfather, Ellis.

It had been a grueling game. I was glad the shot went in because it gave us a victory. I was so exhausted I do not think I could have played a second overtime.

* * *

Dad had always told me not to practice shots from any-where on the floor I did not expect to shoot from in a game. He and Mom were waiting in the gym when I left the dressing room that night. I went over to the spot where I launched the shot, looked at Dad and said:

"No point in shooting from here in practice. I'll never do it in a game." He tried to hide his reaction, but I think a smile did cross his face.

* * *

After that South squeaker, we came back the next night to defeat Mitchell, our rivals from across White River, 60-43. We were perfect on the season, 12-0, highly ranked and we had a week to prepare for our game at Bloomfield against the Cardinals.

Bloomfield was unranked, but it did have an outstanding player in Mike Sherrard. We were ahead 10 points with 7 minutes to play when our game went sour. Bloomfield came back strong to win, 66-64.

Coach Bush was upset and he had reason to be livid. We had allowed a team to outscore us 30-13 in 8 minutes. We had done it with poor shot selections, missed free throws, turnovers and poor defense.

I missed five of 11 free throws and hit only nine of 17 field goal attempts. I took the loss hard, putting much of the blame on my shoulders.

If my teammates were to look to me as the best player, I would have to do better than that. If the media, fans and coaches were going to cite me for outstanding games in victories, I expected them to blame me for not playing well in losses. If I was going to get part of the glory, I was going to have to share the heat. I did not have a problem with that.

I stood up in the locker room before we showered and told the players: "I appreciate you getting me the ball. You got it to me tonight, but I let you down. I will not let you down again."

Once the coach saw I was as unhappy as he was, he patted me on the back, saying we did not lose the game because of me. His compassion did not alleviate the loss, but it helped.

We would not lose again until the State Finals. We bounced back quickly defeating Seymour, 66-57, and Brownstown, 80-48. We did not savor the Brownstown victory, however, because

Speer, our inside man, injured his knee and would be out of action for weeks.

It was fortunate we had a week to prepare for Jeffersonville, a talented team led by Paris Bryant and James Lewis. That interim allowed Noel to work into Speer's spot.

I remember we were down 13 points before coming back to trail 77-74. Boshears, a reserve, drove the baseline for a bucket and a few seconds later hit me with a perfect pass for a basket. We went ahead to win, 81-77.

Critics were claiming we were a one-man team, but a reserve had come off the bench to show we had depth. I did score 38 points in the game, but my teammates had helped secure the victory.

Coach Bush despises errors and we eliminated all except one in a 69-67 victory over Floyd Central that gave us another Hoosier Hills Conference championship. In that game I took a career high 29 shots, made 15 for 42 points. I also had 12 rebounds.

We closed the regular season with victories over Martinsville, Evansville Central and Columbus East. In that Columbus game, Brent Byrer lofted a pass that allowed me to score the first alley oop basket of my career.

Someone told me later that I had broken Scott Turner's BNL scoring record, but I was more interested in victories than in records.

Once again our regular season had been successful. We were 19-1 but felt we should have been 20-0. The team chemistry had been even better than the previous year. Speer never fully recovered from his injury and his loss hurt our depth even though Noel had played well at center.

* * *

Fans clamored for tickets to the Seymour sectional where the draw indicated we would have to defeat Jennings County, Brownstown and Seymour for the second time that year to win a spot in the regional. In Indiana basketball few victories come easy.

I took the Jennings County game personally. I had been bottled up in our earlier meeting and I was convinced I would not let that happen again. Our picks allowed me to get free from the defense, then get the ball for drives to the basket.

We won, 72-59, and thanks to my teammates who allowed me to get open, I scored 33 points. I did not have a particularly good game against Brownstown, but Pittman did. He scored 21 points in the 90-60 victory, another indication that we had players other than me who could score.

Seymour already was growing tired of our dominance in its gym and was eager for an upset. It was not to be. We defeated the Owls, 85-74, in a game in which I scored 47 points.

I was pleased, however, to hear Seymour coach Gary Merrell praised our entire team. "A lot of credit," he said, "should go to the team as a whole. Byrer, Pittman and Ritter all played with poise. That is their strong point."

In a week we would be back at Seymour to defend our regional title.

* * *

Despite mergers, some small schools still remain among the giant consolidations, hoping to become modern Milans, dreaming of a sequel to the movie "Hoosiers." New Washington was one of those Davids, primed and ready to slay the Goliaths of the late 1980s. It had three of the better players in southern Indiana in Shannon Arthur and Scott and Jamie Matthews, twin sons of Coach Jim Matthews.

The Mustangs would be our afternoon opponent in the regional.

New Washington had 262 students compared to the 1,800-plus at BNL, making us the heavy favorites. Chances are some fans had mixed emotions as the game began. We had won a loyal following throughout southern Indiana, but hundreds of those fans had attended small schools in their youth and still remembered their own dreams of glory.

New Washington had proved its mettle over the season and stayed close for three quarters. We managed to win 73-62, but it had not been an easy victory.

That game set up a rematch with Jeffersonville, a team that had taken us to the limit in mid-season on the Red Devils floor. We had an easier time winning the return game, 91-68. It was another one of those nights when my shots fell, 18 of 24 from the field, 15 of 17 from the foul line, for a high school career-high 51 points.

We had another regional championship and some more net to clip from the goals at the Seymour gym, which we were beginning to consider our second home.

The semistate was ahead. We would be playing at Hulman Center on the campus of Indiana State University at Terre Haute for the first time. That was where Larry Bird played his college ball. I was looking forward to playing on the same floor for he was a person I greatly admired.

* * *

Our first opponent in the semistate would be Loogootee, a team directed by crafty Jack Butcher, one of the winningest coaches in Indiana basketball.

We expected a tough game and the Lions gave us one, keeping the game close through three quarters. I think it was early in the fourth quarter when I chased down a loose ball and took it to the hoop for a two-handed dunk. That seemed to give us the momentum we needed to secure a 72-63 victory.

I finished that game with 30 points and 10 rebounds, but I was more concerned about our opponent in the night game.

We had expected to play Evansville Central, but the Bears were upset in the afternoon by Greencastle, a team that was making its first appearance in the Sweet Sixteen in two decades.

Fans thought Central had cinched victory when it scored to take a 61-59 lead with five seconds to play. Little is certain in basketball, however. Greencastle made two crisp passes, allow-ing Chad Remsburg to drive the baseline and tie the game.

In the overtime, Central had possession and a 65-61 lead with 58 seconds to play. One of its players, instead of laying the ball in the basket, went for a dunk and missed. A Greencastle trey was followed by a steal and the Tiger Cubs went on to win 69-65.

I mentioned that game for two reasons. One is that opponents should never be taken lightly. The other is that dunks may please fans, but a player who tries one had better make darn sure it goes in the basket.

Fans who thought Greencastle would be exhausted after that game were wrong. It came back strong that night, any weariness offset by dreams of an upset. Doug Miller, the Greencastle coach, had his team in a box-and-one defense, which held us to a 42-38 lead at the end of the third quarter. I had 11 points at that time.

The Greencastle players may have begun to tire or we may have decided to shift gears. I scored 13 straight points in the fourth quarter and we won, 62-47.

I always seemed to score a lot of points in high school in the fourth quarter. In reflection, I think a big reason for that was because of the importance I placed on conditioning. I ran every morning before school and made an effort to be in better shape than my opponents. This was one of those games when that effort and dedication made a difference.

A player may not reap the benefits of conditioning tomorrow or next week, but somewhere down the line it will pay off. It did for me in this case.

That Greencastle victory gave us another semistate championship. Another trip to Market Square Arena was ahead. We again had met the expectations of our fans.

* * *

School was out for spring break again that year so once again we avoided some of the distractions that would have come had we been in class. We were able instead to concentrate on our opponent, Muncie Central, a powerhouse in Indiana basketball seeking its eighth state championship.

The Bearcats, coached by Bill Harrell and led by Chandler Thompson, were out of the North Central Conference, which sports writers called the strongest in the state. We wanted to prove that the Hoosier Hills league was just as good.

Fans throughout the state saw us as small town kids, related to us, wished us well. If the 17,490 fans in Market Square had voted we would have won. Fans may stir a team to greater heights, but the players have to win the games.

We started strong, leading 8-0, before Coach Harrell called a timeout. The game stayed close from then on, but we never could get over the hump and take control again. We lost 60-53, a defeat that was as painful as the loss to Marion a year earlier.

Chandler Thompson, an all-state player who went on to star at Ball State, was unstoppable. I scored 25 points and had nine rebounds, but Chandler's game was much better. He scored 32 points, many on disheartening slam dunks and obviously was the star of the game.

That night Central went on to crush Concord, and its star Shawn Kemp, 76-53, for the state title. Once again we had been bumped from the tournament by the eventual state champion. The title had been within reach, but we had not grasped it.

Our season was over. We were 26-2 for the year. I had added 872 points to my scoring total for a 31.1 point per game average and had averaged nine rebounds. Again I would be named to all-state teams, but I still did not have a state championship.

On the bus ride home I began to look ahead to the next season. We would lose Pittman, Ritter, Noel, Speer and some senior reserves. Those of us who returned and those who wanted to move up from the junior varsity would need to work hard in the off season, which is the best time for players to improve their individual skills.

I was, however, ready for a respite. My knees had begun to bother me and I had not had a summer off from basketball since I was eight years old.

PART VII

FRUSTRATION SEASON

That summer was the first time in five years I did not play on an AAU team. I tried to stay in shape while letting the knee heal, but I did not compete in games and I did not run much.

I did not do anything as far as basketball was concerned. I think that took away from my game, robbed me of my feel for it. That may have been an omen of the season to come.

While I relaxed, Ray Manis, the BNL athletic director, and Coach Bush were busy. Our own fieldhouse was sold out for the season. Few of the schools we were to face on the road could accommodate the crowds that wanted to see us play.

The attention we were attracting had become a circus and we needed big tops under which to accommodate the crowds.

Manis and Bush approved site changes for six of our 10 roads, including one at the 16,910-seat Market Square Arena in Indianapolis. That meant we would play before almost 150,000 fans during the regular season.

* * *

When practice started in October, Coach Bush was looking for three starters to replace Jay Ritter, Greg Pittman and Brad Noel, who had graduated.

In a pre-season assessment, he said, "We're very inexperienced. I look at our schedule and it's kind of frightening. We'll either get good exposure or get exposed." That did not keep "Hoosier Basketball" magazine from rating us No. 13 in its pre-season rating.

It did not take Coach Bush too long to settle on a starting lineup. Jamie Cummings and Jimmy Jones moved into the spots vacated by Pittman and Ritter. Jason Lambrecht took over at center for Noel and Jeff Speer. Byrer and I stayed at the forward positions.

I was not certain what to expect and chances are neither did the coaching staff. Whatever! We started the season at home with a roar over the Salem Lions, winning 80-55. I remember after scoring 50 points in that game, Coach Bush said he had seen me have better games, then added:

"Not that he played poorly, because he played hard and the other kids got him the ball in the right spots."

Playing hard was what the game was all about and it was good to see Jones, Cummings and Lambrecht, the new starters, be part of the action. I hit 17 of 29 shots in that game, the most attempts of my high school career.

Our next game against Bloomington North had been moved to Market Square Arena, giving fans, who did not have tickets to home games, a chance to see us play.

My shot was as off target as it had been on against Salem. I hit only 6 of 21 shots, my worst average in high school, and 7 of 13 free throws. I did pull down 11 rebounds and took two charges late in the game that were big plays. It was another night I would realize there are other ways to help my team than score.

We won the low-scoring game, 41-37. Incidentally, one of the North players was Pat Knight, the son of I.U. Coach Bob Knight.

* * *

I had grown up watching Indiana University teams, had dreamed—like almost every kid in southern Indiana does—of playing there for Coach Knight. We lived 20 miles from Assembly Hall, an easy drive for my parents and grandparents.

Knight had indicated through his attendance at games and his letters that he wanted me to play for him.

I had almost two full years of high school left, but it had always been in my mind that I would play for Indiana. I never considered any other school seriously although I did visit Purdue and talked with Gene Keady. To Purdue's credit, it did not persist when it became obvious I had my mind set on I.U.

I remembered Steve Alford's advice: "Commit once you are positive where you want to play." I was now certain, told my parents, then Coach Bush. I did not consider my decision to be a major news story but some papers used the announcement on page 1 or to lead the sports sections.

I told sports writers then, "I know I will have to work hard. I am willing to make that sacrifice. Even if I don't play much, it'll be a real experience." How much of an "experience" it would be, I did not know at the time.

From then on I was free of recruiting distractions. No one tried to get me to change my mind even though I had made only a verbal commitment and had no legal obligation except my word which I would not have broken regardless of any incentives that might have been offered. I think, even then, coaches knew me well enough to know I would not renege on a pledge.

That decision made, I could play without the distractions that come with being wooed by recruiters. The calls and letters stopped and any coaches that came to see our games were there to see the game, not to recruit me.

Patrick Knight would be the only other freshman on the I.U. team when I enrolled at Indiana in August, 1990.

* * *

It was not obvious that I had been freed from the pressure of recruiters the next game. It may have appeared I had my mind somewhere else. We barely eased by the Hatchets at Washington, 56-53, in a game in which I hit just 9 of 22 shots and finished with 21 points and 11 rebounds. Byrer led the scoring with 25, so the two of us combined for all except 10 of our points

My knees were bothering me and I had trouble with my shots. I was not playing up to my expectations and neither was the team.

We made our first trip to storied Hinkle Fieldhouse on the Butler University campus in Indianapolis for the Bloomington

South game. I remember Jones looked around the gym and said, "It's old. It looks like something from Heltonville."

South still had the big redhead, Chris Lawson, who also was headed for Indiana. He had 19 points, but we had better balance. Byrer had 16, Jimmy and I had 14 each, and we won 59-52.

That quieted the "one-man team" comments briefly. I was pleased when Coach Bush told reporters, "Damon doesn't care if he gets 50 or 2 as long as his team wins. You will notice his team wins most of the time."

He knew I wanted to be a winner, not a one-man team. We proved others could score the next game when we rolled over Madison, 88-59. Jones and Byrer had 21 each and I added 20 points and eight assists. I was still unhappy with my shooting, hitting only 8 of 19 attempts.

My shooting eye was better the next outing when we thumped Perry Meridian, 81-49, in a game played in the 7,248-seat Southport fieldhouse. I drilled 10 of 19 attempts from the field and finished with 28 points. My eight assists led to 16 more in what I thought was my first really good outing since the Salem opener.

We were unbeaten, rising each week in the polls. That was all the incentive a good Edgewood team needed to play one of its best games of the season. Fans thought we had finally subdued the Mustangs when we took a 56-46 lead. They were too optimistic too soon. Four Edgewood three-pointers cut the margin to 73-72 with five seconds left to play. Edgewood had a chance to go ahead on a one-and-one free throw situation. Eric Flinn, a reserve, was fouled on the rebound and he hit both his chances, letting us escape with a 75-72 victory.

We had needed all of my 41 points to win. They came on 18 of 24 field goal attempts. My shot was back, which was a relief as we headed into the Christmas break, which would be inter-rupted by another trip to Hinkle Fieldhouse to play Carmel.

I had played five high school games in Indianapolis and had never had what I considered anything better than an average game. I knew some fans in the state capital thought I was overrated so I was determined to do better when we met the Greyhounds on a foggy night shortly after Christmas.

It was one of those nights every player hopes for. We rolled to a 78-47 victory. I had 34 points on 9 of 17 field goal attempts and 8 of 10 free throws and was credited with 13 rebounds.

That extra time I had spent working on my shot had paid off. I felt comfortable, confident when I released the ball. It felt like it was going in when I shot. When that happens, it is a great feeling for a player.

We were unbeaten, 8-0, but the new year would bring tougher competition. My knees bothered me, Byrer's knees bothered him. There were times the pains were so severe we would not practice. We looked ahead, our anticipation mixed with apprehension.

After cruising past Jennings County, 73-45, we traveled to Terre Haute where Coach Pat Rady and his South Braves were waiting to avenge that overtime loss the previous season.

South had what Rady considered his best team ever, a roster that included veteran Tony McGee, Steve Richardson, Rowdy Williams, a four-year starter who later would play at Franklin College, and 6-10 Jim Deister.

We were down by 11 at one point, but came back to tie the game at 47-47, then went ahead on a pair of free throws by Derek Clouse. We lost that lead when Richardson drilled a three-point shot and South went on to win, 52-48.

The statistics showed I had 24 points and 10 rebounds. I would remember the loss a lot longer than those figures.

We defeated Mitchell, 94-65, and gained revenge for the previous season's loss at Bloomfield with an 85-48 victory over the Cardinals at the BNL fieldhouse. I shot well in those two games, scoring 35 against Mitchell and 25 in the Bloomfield game when I also had 13 rebounds.

We knew Seymour would be primed for an upset the next week. We had won nine straight games there, including two sectional titles, and the Owls were eager to end that streak.

They were ahead, I recall, at the end of the third quarter before clutch shooting by Jones and Byrer bailed us out, 60-55.

My game was so-so, 16 points on 8 of 15 shooting. It was the first game in my career I did not shoot a single free throw. I took five three-point shots and missed all of them.

The next night we routed Brownstown, 65-40. I did not shoot well, scoring 18 points on 8 of 19 attempts, but did have 13 rebounds for the third time that season.

We were 13-1 now and the most difficult part of the season was ahead, including four conference games. Most of the teams we had faced had slowed the games and concentrated on keeping the ball out of our hands as much as possible.

That is why we looked forward to our next game against Jeffersonville. The Red Devils liked to go all-out, end-to-end from start to finish, more intent on offense than defense. It would be a welcome change from the pace we had played most of the season.

We rolled to a surprisingly easy 97-69 victory. Everyone played well, especially Byrer who scored 21 and Jason Lambrecht who had 20 to go with my 23 markers. I also had a season-high 10 assists, mainly because Brent and Jason seemed to score each time I got them the ball. Our defense was as good as the offense, leading to 26 Jeffersonville errors.

I remember thinking that run-and-shoot game was a lot of fun. I would have thought differently had we lost.

We were unbeaten in the Hoosier Hills Conference. That would not last long. Our next game was at Floyd Central, which had Pat Graham, twins Shane and Sean Gibson and Todd Howard. It was the most solid team we would face all season.

Graham was outstanding as usual, scoring 31 points. We stayed close, despite his shooting and rebounding, and had a chance to win on a three-point shot that caromed off the rim. The final score was Floyd Central 67, BNL 65.

Byrer matched my 21 points, proving once again we had other players who could score. That did not seem important at the time. We had lost the game and we would not have a chance to meet the Highlanders again unless we won the Seymour sectional.

I had shot under .500 from the field for three straight games. The season was nearing an end and I needed to regain my touch. I cannot recall for sure, but it probably was one of those times when Dad took me to the gym at Heltonville to correct what I was doing wrong.

My shot returned as quickly as it departed. I netted 14 of 20 shots for 35 points in a 63-53 victory over New Albany.

Coach Knight found a seat for himself and Dick Vitale, the television commentator, at our home game against Martinsville. I had learned to concentrate on the game, not the crowd. I shot well again, hitting 15 of 18 shots for 37 markers in an 89-51 victory.

* * *

That Martinsville game was the only time I was called for a technical for anything other than hanging on the rim. I was bumped by a couple of Martinsville defenders on a fast break and I swung my arms to keep from falling. The official who called the "T" thought I was trying to elbow one of the defenders.

A couple of Martinsville players gave me some lip while their teammate shot the technical foul. I did not forget it. We went into a full court man-to-man press the next time the Artesians had possession under our basket. When the ball came inbound to one of the Martinsville players who had done the trash talking, he waved his hands to signal his teammates to clear out so he could bring the ball upcourt alone. There was no way I was going to allow him to do that. I stole the ball from him, passed it to Cummings who scored and was fouled for a 3-point play.

Two years later Coach Knight asked me what I thought was the greatest play he had seen me make in high school. I shook my head. It was that steal after the technical and the trash talk, he said.

* * *

We closed the regular season, defeating Evansville Central, 71-48, and Columbus East, 90-50, in a game in which I scored 40 points, the most since that opening game 50 against Salem.

We were 18-2 going into the sectional. We had exceeded the expectations of pollsters and critics. Our fans, however, wanted to make a third straight trip to the State Finals. So did we.

Again tickets for the Seymour regional were a premium. Our fans sought any the smaller schools, Medora and Crothersville, might not sell. Few, if any, were available.

We defeated Crothersville, 64-30, in the opener when guard Jones had nine steals. That victory set up a rematch with Seymour, a team that had played us close during the regular season.

We took no chances against the Owls this time, jumping ahead 18-8 en route to a 77-58 victory. I was 12 of 17 from the field and 8 of 11 from the free throw line for 33 points.

Starting with the New Albany game I had hit 78 of 111 field goals, a .700 average. I am not exactly sure what I had done, other than regain confidence in my shot. I was more concerned about what kind of defense Coach Joe Null would throw at me when we faced Jennings County for the sectional title.

It was not just one defense but several. The Panthers stopped me, but not my teammates, and we were on our way to another championship when I broke the small finger on my left hand attempting to deflect a pass.

It was painful, but I did not want to detract from the 92-64 victory or the celebration on the floor. I had scored a season-low 13 points, but Byrer had a game-high 27, Lambrecht added 17 and Cummings 12. It had been a team victory and I could wait a few minutes to be concerned about my finger.

There was a third-straight sectional championship to savor, nets to be cut, a few moments to enjoy.

Coach Bush often said that every time I coughed all of Bedford caught a cold. If that was the case, a lot of people may have had an ache in their little finger.

I was treated in Indianapolis by Dr. James Strickland and fitted with a brace designed to protect the finger. I was confident I could play and Floyd Central coach Joe Hinton made me feel even better. Hinton in a pre-game assessment, said, "I'm sure it will hurt him, but he can play with pain. The only way the game will be even is if I get on the floor with my kids. Damon is a coach on the floor."

Like Coach Bush, Hinton was a competitor. I was happy he saw me as one, too.

That Floyd Central game was a classic, close from start to finish. Each time we fell behind, we fought back. We trailed after three quarters, 54-49, then rallied for a 65-65 deadlock to send the game into overtime.

Graham came off a pick early in the extra period, then launched an arching bomb from 25 feet out that floated through the net. He came back with a two-pointer to give the Highlanders a 70-65 lead and we never recovered, losing, 75-72.

Graham, who also was headed for I.U., scored 38 points. I had 37 and seven rebounds.

It had been a game that exemplifies what basketball is all about. It is the competition that drives players. Win or lose, that competition is why you play the game. If you cannot tolerate losing, you do not deserve to win.

That loss, nevertheless, was hard to accept. We realized, however, we were defeated by a good team. If we had to lose, we were grateful it was to a talented team that deserved to win.

It would be a March when we would not travel to Indianapolis in search of a state title. Our fans returned home disappointed, but no more so than the players.

* * *

We finished the season 21-3, not bad for a team that had started the year with three new players in the starting lineup. I had scored 653 points, moving my high school total to 2,162 and would again be named to the all-state team. I was disappointed, nevertheless.

The season had its frustrations. My knees hurt, I had trouble with my shot at times and I never really thought I got going as a player or we got going as a team. Neither Byrer nor I practiced much at times, hoping to protect our knees as much as possible. That may have hurt us as a team.

I know I was not at all pleased with the way I played or the way we performed as a team. I do not know what it was. Maybe it was the talent or the chemistry. I do not think the players understood their roles as well as members of our other BNL teams knew their responsibilities.

Looking back in the perspective of hindsight, I would say that was my worst season in high school. I might have thought differently had we won and gone further in the tournament. One loss can detract from a lot of victories.

That loss to Floyd Central, that season of frustration would set the stage for a better year to come.

* * *

Floyd Central remained in the tournament until losing, 73-70, to Kokomo in the afternoon game of the State Finals. Pat Graham won the Trester Award and later would be named Mr. Basketball.

PART VIII

ROAD TO THE TOP

In three years our BNL teams had an enviable 70-9 record, one of the best in the state. I was not satisfied and neither was Coach Bush.

I had set three goals when I entered BNL, to win a state championship, to be Mr. Basketball and to be recruited as a player by a major university. I had committed to I.U., but I still did not have a state championship and the voting for Mr. Basketball was months away.

Our fans deserved a state title. They had filled the gym each time we played, had outnumbered some of our opponents' home fans when we went on the road. We had been to the state finals twice, but close was not good enough. I had one more year, one last season to help a team win the title for Coach Bush and those fans.

Before school was out my junior year, I asked Marc Anderson, the varsity football coach, for a weight regimen I could follow during the summer. I had been bumped around by opponents that season and I was intent on not letting it happen again.

It was a mind set I kept for the entire season to come. If I was going to realize a dream I had one year to do it. I knew we would need to dedicate ourselves to that goal, not only during the season but during our summer vacation as well.

We—me and the team members who were expected to play a lot—worked out often during those hot months. We played in open gym at BNL, drove up to I.U. and competed against college kids, scrimmaged against Dad and other adults in the gym at Heltonville. It was something we did on our own because the coaching staff could not be involved under Indiana High School Athletic Association rules.

Summer passes slowly for basketball players who live for the game. That summer of 1989 was no different, despite those nightly workouts. We were eager to get on with the challenge that was ahead.

* * *

During the summer, the IHSAA had announced the 1990 State Finals would be held in the Hoosier Dome which would be configured to seat 41,046 fans. Skeptics doubted it would be filled, ending decades of state final sellouts.

Coach Bush had been at the press conference when the announcement was made. At the first practice that October he unfolded a T-shirt with a picture of the dome and "State Finals— March 24, 1990" printed on it.

"That's where I want to be next March 24," he said. That is where we dedicated ourselves to take him, as a coach, not as a spectator.

He shifted his eyes toward the roof of the fieldhouse and added, "And I'd like to see a state championship banner up there." His goals were our goals.

We had lost Brent Byrer, a big part of our team for three years, and Jimmy Jones, a one-year starter, plus reserves Derek Clouse, Eric Flinn, Reno Bates and Greg Mahuron.

Coach Bush added his son, Alan, and Chad Mills, Dwayne Curry, Ethan Cox, Paul Stevens, Ryan Moutardier and Brent Conner to the returning roster.

I was the only one who had been to the State Finals so it was up to me to lead them there, then be successful once we arrived.

It was time for me to show a different kind of leadership. I had tried to lead by example, by hard work and hustle, by doing what the coach asked. Now it was time to be vocal, to let the others know their roles, to be a coach on the floor.

I was not sure that was the most talented team we had. To succeed it would have to be through effort and dedication. It was soon obvious that no group was smarter, more willing to work.

As individuals they grasped their roles quickly, did what they could do well, did not try to play beyond their limitations.

Players who were scorers shot the ball, rebounders rebounded, passers passed, defenders defended, reserves did what they were expected to do. It was amazing how each player grasped his role. We certainly would not be the best five players in Indiana, but we were determined to be the best team.

Coach Bush noticed that I was more focused, even more dedicated, than ever.

At practices, he insisted, "We will get the ball to No. 32. We will get it to him. We will get it to him." I was No. 32. I did not want to do all the shooting. but I knew I would need to offset part of the scoring Byrer had done the previous year.

By the time the season started, Curry was in Jones' spot at guard, Chad Mills at forward, replacing Byrer. Alan Bush proved in practice he would be one of our top reserves.

Our fans were delighted the opener had been moved to Seymour, a gym with a lot more seats than the one at Salem.

We were impatient, as they were, for the season to begin. The suspense did not last long. We led 36-8 after a quarter and went on to win, 92-36. Alan Bush proved he could play at our level, hitting four straight three-point shots and scoring 16 points. Salem coach Jim Irwin may have overstated my contribution.

"Damon," he said, "is so much better than anyone in the world. You saw an Indiana legend. He had 35 points, but he could have had 135."

When the polls came out a few days later, we were ranked fifth in the state.

We returned home to meet Bloomington North, which always seemed to play its best games against us. The Cougars were ahead, 50-48, before we overtook them for a hard-earned 64-55 victory. I hit 14 of 20 shots for 37 points which moved me into sixth place on the list of all-time scorers in Indiana high school basketball.

I still was more concerned about the team and victories than about any personal glory. The countdown to the scoring record had started and fans were estimating when I might break the old mark.

My goal was to be a complete player and I think the next game against Washington proved I was or, at least, could be one. I was credited with 14 assists, the most I had at that point, collected 11 rebounds and scored 23 points. Four other players scored in double figures and two others added nine points each in the 93-55 romp.

Our next game against Bloomington South was an old-time southern Indiana barnburner. We won, 88-82, by shooting a torrid .632 from the field. Jason Lambrecht was 10 for 10, much better than my 16 of 26 which was good for 37 points.

I do not recall much about our 92-45 win over Perry Meridian except that I went up over 6-6 Doug Fites for a stuff that delighted fans. The scorebook showed I had scored 39 points.

We then defeated Edgewood, 105-75, a game in which we netted 16 of 24 three-point shots. Alan Bush hit seven of 11 from behind the arc and I was six of eight to finish with 36 points despite being sick earlier in the week.

In the showers after the game, Alan said congratulations. I asked, "For what?" He said, "For breaking the school record for 3-pointers in a game." He paused for a while, then added, "By the way, I broke your record."

* * *

I believe that was the night Marion Pierce, who held the high school career scoring record, was in the crowd. He had set the mark of 3,019 in 1961 playing for Lewisville, a small school that later became a part of Tri High in Henry County. Fans were certain I might break that standard if we went far enough in the tournament.

Pierce, I think, had mixed emotions. I am sure he was hoping his record would stand, but I sensed he was pleased to be back in the spotlight after 30 years even if he dropped to second place.

* * *

Christmas was just six days away. We were a perfect 6 and 0. I was happy with the way the team was playing, pleased that my game was much more consistent than it had been the previous year. I was averaging 34.5 points a game and shooting .640.

I knew I would need to score points for this team to win and that is what I tried to do. The other players were getting me the ball and Alan Bush was opening up the inside with his three-point shooting.

We looked forward to a short Christmas break, knowing that three big games in four days would follow the holiday. Two of those would be in the Hall of Fame Classic at Assembly Hall at Bloomington, where in a year I would be playing for the Hoosiers.

Skeptics came from across the state for the classic, many doubting our BNL team was as good as its press clippings. We were ranked No. 3, were about to face a Pike team that was No. 2. Those who had not seen us play expected a Pike victory.

Pike may have been the most talented team in the state that year. It had LaSalle Thompson, Marcus Johnson and Lloyd Carr, who was on our Municipal Gardens AAU teams.

The Red Devils had us down 39-34 at the half and it appeared the skeptics were right. Coach Bush was not convinced. "You haven't played well," he said, "but you are still in the game."

Alan Bush was struggling with his shot. When Johnson, the 6-9 Pike center was called for hanging on the rim, I told Alan to shoot the technical, even though I was the designated shooter.

When he walked to the line with the ball, Coach Bush yelled to me: "WHAT are you doing?" The "what" seemed to be in capital letters. I walked to the sidelines, explained that we needed to get Alan involved in the game and that I felt the free throw would give him some confidence.

Alan made the free toss. I was off the hook with the coach, who said it was hard to argue with my logic because his son was an .850 shooter at the foul line.

That free toss helped us win, 65-60. Team play, smartness, desire and heart had offset talent. I scored 31 points and had 13 rebounds but it was a game in which each player carried out the role he was assigned.

I knew that if we were going to be a solid team Alan would have to be a big part in what we were doing. He would have to shoot the ball and shoot it well. I was just trying to get him started.

That was something I tried to do that entire season. I tried to help make each player better, tried to make them realize what we needed to do to win the state championship.

I could have stepped up to the foul line and probably added another point to my career total. That point record was not what I was all about. The records, the points, all those things are nice. But our goal of winning the state championship was more important.

That night we faced Lawrence North, the defending state champions who still had Eric Montross, my 7-foot friend who had played on our AAU teams. It was the first time we had met as foes.

The game was tied 50-50 when Montross hit a free throw with 6 seconds to play. I was unable to get off a shot before the clock ran out and we lost 51-50. I had 26 points, but hit only 8 of 21 shots, the first time in eight games I had shot under .500 from the field.

We had not played poorly. "We simply didn't shoot the ball well," Coach Bush explained.

Back at BNL, the coach talked to us for 15 or 20 minutes. Jamie and I, the "old men" on the team, then talked about that long. I said, "They won. We lost by a single point. It's not a big deal. That state tournament is what counts."

Sure, I hated to lose. But these were the hardest working kids I had played with at BNL. I wanted to keep their expectations at a high level. I felt good about our chances.

Two nights later we met Carmel at Hinkle Fieldhouse. I knew some fans in Indianapolis still thought I was overrated. I wanted to change that and I wanted to make sure we won the game so the younger players would regain any lost confidence from the Lawrence North loss.

This time the shots did fall for an 88-73 victory. I hit 17 of 19 attempts, many of which were set up by sharp passes from my teammates. My 42 points were a season high and moved me past Billy Shepherd into fourth place on the all-time scoring list. Shepherd's son Scott, ironically, had 31 for Carmel.

A few days later we were ranked No. 1 in the state United Press International poll.

The lofty ranking may have subconsciously gone to our heads. We opened 1990 with a game at Jennings County that did not please Coach Bush. We won, 62-40, but he complained, "I was not pleased in any way, shape or form. It's not often you can say this about these kids, but they didn't come ready to play tonight."

I am not sure but I suppose he included me in that assessment. I scored 23 points, tying my lowest output to that point in the season.

We started the next game slowly, too, trailing Terre Haute South at the half, then played better the rest of the way to win, 68-55. Brian Evans, who would later play at I.U., scored 19 for the Braves. I had 38 points and 10 rebounds.

In an 84-46 victory over Mitchell, I recorded another triple double, 24 points, 13 rebounds and 12 assists. Paul Stevens came off the bench to score 14 points. Our reserves were becoming a bigger part of each victory.

After fairly easy victories over Bloomfield, 70-33, and Seymour, 89-67, we were at Brownstown for a Saturday night game no one would soon forget.

I did not play well or shoot well early in the game which allowed Brownstown to take a lead and gain confidence. It was a game in which a small school was determined to compete with a ranked team, knowing a victory would be a topic of conversation for decades.

The Braves were ahead, as they had been much of the game, when I hit a jumper with 3 seconds left to tie the game, 50-50. I did not think it was a three-pointer, which would have won the game, although some BNL fans did.

The first overtime was even wilder. Brownstown appeared to have the game won, leading by four points with 16 seconds to play when one of its players went to the free-throw line for one-and-bonus. Coach Bush admitted later he thought victory was beyond our grasp. That changed quickly.

The shooter missed the free throw, I was bumped attempting to retrieve the loose ball, a personal foul was called and I hit two free throws. When Brownstown inbounded the ball, Cummings stepped in the passing lane, slapped the ball to me and I hit what I thought was a three-pointer. It was called a two, however, leaving the score knotted, 56-56.

Alan Bush hit a three in the second overtime and we added seven of eight free throws for a 66-60 victory.

I scored 37 points and had 12 rebounds but it was a team victory, one that had not come easily. The outcome had fans from both schools looking forward to a rematch in the Seymour sectional.

Coach Bush reviewed the tapes later and said the referees had made the right calls on the two shots that were questioned. My foot had been on the three-point line each time.

.* * *

By then I was beginning to sense that this could be the team that could win the state championship. I was even more convinced after we defeated Jeffersonville on the road, 85-81. We could have lost to both Brownstown and Jeffersonville. Both were hard-fought games we had to pull together to win. I was scoring well (adding 36 against Jeffersonville) and the players had accepted their roles and were executing them better each game.

We defeated Floyd Central, 85-61, and Madison, 71-51, for 17-1 record going into a Hoosier Hills conference game at New Albany.

* * *

Gary Austin, the New Albany athletic director, joked before the game that it was the "biggest thing since the 1937 flood, maybe bigger."

Some writers considered Coach Jim Miller's ranked Bulldogs the best team in southern Indiana. We were 17-1, riding a

10-game winning streak. The game was telecast in the Louisville area and some BNL fans, who did not have tickets, checked in at motels to watch.

None of those TV viewers turned to a suspense movie. The game had more drama. Neither team could take command until New Albany eased in front 60-57 with seconds to go. Coach Miller ordered his team to foul me as soon as I got the ball, preventing a possible three-point shot.

I went to the foul line with about 2 seconds remaining. Our only hope was to make the first shot, miss the second and hope for a rebound basket that would tie the score. I made the first shot and tried to miss the second, but banked it in. We lost 60-59. I had 30 points, one of which I would rather not have had.

I did not know until later that I had passed Arley Andrews as the No. 2 all-time scorer in Indiana. The news was little consolation.

It was late when we returned through the rain and fog to the BNL gym. We were due in Martinsville for a Saturday game in a few hours. That did not stop us from having another team meeting. We did not want a loss on the road to an outstanding New Albany team to detract us from our objective.

Martinsville stayed close most of the game before we won, 82-69. Our bench once again showed its versatility. This time it was reserve Ethan Cox who came in to score nine points and help shut down the Artesians' front line. I had 32 points in that game and again the following week when we defeated Central at Evansville, 77-47. I also had a season-high 15 assists and 13 rebounds against Central, giving me my third triple double of the season.

* * *

Our regular season was about to end. Our final home game at Bedford North Lawrence was a week away against Columbus East. In four years we had won 38 and lost none on our home court.

The finale was an emotional time for me and the other seniors, as are most farewells. We tried to stay focused, knowing

East had won some big games during the season, had quality players such as Lance Barker.

Sports writers from the *New York Times* and *Sports Illustrated* were there as were reporters from Indianapolis, Louisville and other cities. Television station helicopters, we were told, had taken over the football field.

It was a situation ripe for an upset and East was determined to spoil our season, dampen the festivities and ruin our farewell. The Olympians were ahead 43-40 in the third quarter when Chad Mills hit a basket and Alan Bush buried a three-pointer. Alan added three more treys in the fourth quarter and we went on to win, 81-75.

I appreciated the comments East Coach Roger Reed made right after the game. "I want to personally congratulate Damon Bailey on a fine high school career. I feel privileged to have coached against him the last four years."

It was good to know I had won the respect of our opponents as well as our backers. I would not learn until later that I had scored 40 points and garnered a season-high 14 rebounds.

Coach Bush kept us on the floor after the game. Almost all of our fans remained as did the East partisans despite the sting of defeat. We appreciated their sportsmanship.

Almost all my former teammates were there, former Stars like Ernie Lovell and Rusty Garrison, who had smoothed the way for me to play as a freshman; Greg Pittman, Jay Ritter and Troy Ikerd, guards on the 1987-88 team; Jimmy Jones and Brent Byrer from the 1988-89 squad.

Those players had been a big part of what we had accomplished over the last four years. I would not have been the player I had become had it not been for them. The hugs I gave each of them as they walked onto the floor in that post-game tribute were sincere.

After each of the other seniors spoke, Coach Bush called me to the microphone, saying I was the best basketball player in the history of Indiana. If that was true, I told the teary-eyed crowd, it was because of all those players who were on the floor with me.

I mentioned that critics had told us for four years that we had no talent on our teams, then reminded those skeptics that we had enough talent to twice reach the Final Four. I added, "We have every intention of going to the Hoosier Dome this year and winning it all."

It also was a time to thank my family. That brought tears to my eyes, choked me up, before I regained my composure to add, "They mean the world to me, everyone of them. All I can say is I love you all very much."

That was a sad time. I had played for four years in front of 6,300 people almost every home game, a 39-game span in which we did not lose. It was difficult to say goodbye to all those people with whom I had so much fun and success. Up to that point, it was my most emotional moment.

Once we finally headed for the dressing room I was surrounded by sports writers with questions I had answered a hundred times. I was still talking to Malcolm Moran of *The New York Times* when the other players headed for home.

I finally had a chance to shower an hour or so later. It was nearing midnight. Coach Bush was still there with a reminder. "Seven o'clock in the morning."

The accolades and the applause had been nice. It was, however, no time to get caught up in sentimentality. It was time to start preparing for post season play. The quest for the brass ring, the gold medallion, that elusive dream I had sought for four years, would start in five days.

* * *

BNL's girls basketball team had a great season, too, and we were at Market Square Arena where it played in the State Finals. It was a day for the girls and I tried to remain inconspicuous and out of the limelight. Some fans still spotted me and asked for autographs.

The girls team defeated Anderson that afternoon, then lost the championship game to Huntington North. If BNL was to have a championship that season, it would be up to the boys team to bring it back from Indianapolis.

ROUND ONE

Lady Luck did not smile on us when the tournament pairings were made. To win the sectional we would, barring upsets, have to beat the three toughest challengers, Brownstown, Jennings County and Seymour.

Sports writers had named us the favorite to capture the state championship. That was nice, but titles are won on the hardwood, not on newsprint.

The favorite label would only make other teams play that much harder against us. No matter! I had confidence in this team and in myself. We were determined.

This was the smartest team I had played with. More than half of us had 3.5 or better grade point indexes. Dwayne Curry had a perfect-plus 4.1. Most were leaders in activities other than basketball.

Each had learned his role well. Each knew what we would need to do in whatever situation that might arise. It was a good feeling knowing what to expect as we prepared to return to Seymour and begin another chase for the championship.

After four years our fans had become adept at finding any available tickets. Many were at the Seymour gym negotiating with scalpers before our bus arrived.

Our rematch with Brownstown had been debated for days. The Braves' fans were hungry for revenge. Our fans were certain this game would not be as suspenseful as our close encounter a few weeks earlier.

It appeared we were in for another battle once the game started. We missed our first seven shots and did not score until Alan Bush came off the bench for a three-pointer. We trailed, 9-8, at the end of the first quarter, hitting just 3 of 14 shots. I had missed five in a row.

I missed another shot before one finally dropped. Ethan Cox came off the bench to hit three baskets and we spurted to a

35-25 lead at the half. We went on to win, 77-55, the first of nine victories we would need to win the state championship.

I scored 26 points but it had been a total team victory. Our bench, led by Alan's 22 points, had scored 40 of our points.

Coach Bush was like my Dad. He knew a team had to do other things when points did not come easily. He appreciated our defense which kept us close until our shots started going in.

* * *

The Jennings County game started the same way. We trailed 7-5 after a quarter. I had been limited to two shots and missed both. Reserves Bush, Cox and Stevens scored our first 12 points.

We turned from frigid to torrid and spurted to a 28-13 lead within a 5-minute period. We went on to win, 82-48. I had 27 points, but again much of the credit went to the reserves. In two games Alan had bombed 12 of 23 from long range and scored 43 points.

Mid-season critics who wondered if he belonged on the team were suddenly silent.

I talked in the dressing room later about the need to rebound and play defense when the shots do not fall, about how important it is to get the entire team involved in the offense.

It may have been the first time I revealed to newsmen my belief that we had a team that could win the state championship.

* * *

Results of season games mean little in tournaments. That did not stop our fans from thinking we would have little trouble with Seymour, a team we had defeated, 89-67, in January.

In four years we were 7-0 against Seymour, winning five of those games on the Owls' floor. New coach Randy Fife wanted to make sure we did not add one more victory to that streak.

We started more quickly against the Owls, hitting 9 of 15 from the field in the first quarter, but Seymour was just as hot. The game remained close and we held a slim 52-51 lead at the end of the third quarter.

The Owls were shooting the lights out. It was unbelievable. Anyone who thought the game would be easy was wrong.

Seymour's defense had clogged up the inside, limiting our shot selection. I told Cummings to start shooting from outside in order to spread the defense. His three-point shots helped do that.

Coach Bush told the team to keep the ball in my hands as much as possible late in the game. I hit seven straight free throws and we hung on to win 69-64. I ended the game with 32 points and Jamie added 16.

It is not often a team shoots .680 from the field and loses. Seymour had done that, hitting 26 of 38 shots, 10 of which were beyond the three-point line. We had won by shooting .571 on 24 of 42 attempts and by improving our interior defense in the second half.

We were very fortunate to pull out that victory. We had our sights on the state championship and we could have easily lost in the sectional. In tournament play in Indiana, nothing can be taken for granted.

With the sectional title secured, the cold I had earlier in the week was forgotten in the excitement that followed.

* * *

Parade Magazine, which appeared in newspapers that Sunday morning, named me to its All-America high school team. Eric Montross, the Lawrence North star, and Alan Henderson, of Brebeuf in Indianapolis, also were on the team.

ROUND TWO

To those who cared, and that seemed almost everyone, I had moved to within 52 points of Marion Pierce's state scoring mark. I was more interested, personally, in the regional than in records.

We would face Charlestown, a big team with a 21-2 record, in the second afternoon game. Our fans assumed we would win and again meet New Albany at night.

We had not looked that far ahead. Coach Bush prepared us for Charlestown, said he would worry about the second game after the first one was over. He had been right to do that. Scottsburg upset New Albany, 48-46, when Chad Marley, a senior guard, drove the baseline for a basket as time ran out.

We built a 40-30 lead over Charlestown, then hit 18 of 20 free throws in the last quarter to win, 65-51. I had scored 28 points to move within 24 of the record. The hoopla that went with that chase for points was becoming a distraction and it would be a relief if, and when, I passed Pierce's total.

* * *

Scottsburg entered the night game with a 22-2 record. We had moved our mark to 25 2. The Warriors had two extra hours of rest, but we were ready to play when the whistle blew.

We were ahead at the half, 32-20, and had control of the game. I was concentrating on the game, not the fans who counted down—"Twenty" ... "Eighteen" ... "Sixteen"—with each basket I scored.

We widened the lead to 53-31 and I was told later some fans were becoming upset because I was looking for the open man, passing off instead of shooting.

At a timeout early in the fourth quarter, student manager Richard Wright, told the team I had tied Pierce's record. Chad Mills suggested we run No. 1, a play where I went back door, caught the ball on a lob pass and slammed it through the basket on a dunk.

Mills made the pass, I grabbed the ball, but two Scottsburg defenders stopped the dunk. I laid the ball against the board for a bank shot. The record had been broken.

The crowd erupted. Play was stopped. The clock, if anyone was watching it, showed 5:55 left in the game. Someone recorded the time. It was 9:25 p.m., March 10, 1990.

Play was held up for 3 minutes so rolls of toilet paper could be cleared from the floor. I rested on the bench, receiving handshakes from teammates who had helped make the record possi-

ble. Scottsburg players added their congratulations. It was grati-
fying to have that kind of response.

It seemed ironic that I had set a new record against
Scottsburg, the team I had scored my first point against 106 games
earlier.

I felt a great burden had been lifted, not that it meant so
much to me at the time. I am glad I got it, but it was not my main
interest at that point in the season.

The record did clear that hurdle, would let us concentrate
on the games ahead, not individual achievement. Fans had
talked about it continually, every newspaper article, almost every
TV sportscast mentioned it. I felt more relieved than excited at
the time. We could move on without that distraction.

The rest of the game was anticlimactic. We went on to win
78-58. I finished that game with 31 points, adding six more
points to the new record the fans had encouraged me to set.

* * *

The next Tuesday I was named the Naismith national basketball player of the year and informed the award would be
made at the Tipoff Club in Atlanta on April 5.

ROUND THREE

We spent the week preparing for our semistate game against
Terre Haute North. North did not have great players. It was a lot
like our team. It played hard, played well, played as a team. We
knew the Patriots would be hard to play against.

For years I had enjoyed competing against teams like that.
Teams that rely on raw talent are not nearly as hard to play
against as those with intelligent players. Teams with smart kids
who know how to play the game are much more difficult to
defeat.

Smart players can make a living playing against talented
individuals who do not understand the game or realize what it
takes to win.

We went to Terre Haute in the team bus the night before the game and stayed at Larry Bird's Boston Connection, a popular hotel during basketball tournaments.

I was the only player on the BNL team who was on the roster two years earlier when we won the semistate at Hulman Center. It would be a new experience for my teammates.

If that bothered us, it did not show. We jumped to a 21-12 lead in the first quarter and were up 38-31 after three quarters. North refused to fold, going on a 23-point rampage and forcing Coach Bush to look to his bench. Paul Stevens came in to score two fielders and five free throws in the last 8 minutes.

We held on for a narrow 56-54 victory. I had been held to 19 points, my lowest total of the season. It was of little concern. We were still in the tournament.

Mark Hisle, a great shooter who would play later at the University of Evansville, had a game-high 24 points. He, too, would have been happier with a victory.

* * *

Evansville Bosse eliminated unbeaten Loogootee, 36-28, in the second game and would be our opponent that night. Bosse was strong, had great individuals who played as a team. Only our best effort would result in victory.

Coach Bush had scribbled a familiar message on the dressing room blackboard: "BNL vs. Bosse. Bosse will be ready. Will BNL?"

This was the semistate. We were one game away from another trip to the State Finals. We were ready. The coach did not take any chances with luck. He wore the same sweater he had worn since our nine-game victory streak started. And, as always, he walked to the scorer's table at exactly 1:00 on the clock to shake hands with BNL scorekeeper Dick McCracken.

Neither team could gain a big advantage and the half ended with Bosse up 35-32. We failed to score during a 3-minute span in the third quarter and fell behind, 45-38. We struggled back for a 50-50 tie. It was Indiana basketball at its best.

Three of Bosse's top players, 6-7 Andy Elkins, 6-5 Ron Darrett, and Antwan Pope, each had been called for four personals. That caused the Bulldogs to go into a zone in an attempt to keep them from fouling out.

Alan Bush, the player I knew we would need to reach the State Finals, drilled a 3-point shot over the zone. He faked Darrett into his fifth foul, then made both free throws and rimmed in another three pointer. We were up 62-58, but Bosse came back to deadlock the game 63-63.

We were clinging to a 67-65 lead when Bush was fouled with 42 seconds to play. "Hit these," I told him, "and we can go to the Dome." He made both shots and I closed out the game with two more free throws for a 72-67 victory.

It had been one of our toughest games of the year, one we could have lost had we not played well. I scored 34 points, including 13 of 14 from the free throw line. I would have been happy to be scoreless had we still won the game.

Alan Bush came into the media room after the game wearing the "State Finals—Hoosier Dome" T-shirt his dad had brought from Indianapolis the previous summer. In a week we would be there, just as the coach had hoped.

I told the sports writers, "Our goal at the beginning of the year was to win the state championship. We're not satisfied to just get there. We have pride in what we have done and what we have accomplished, but we think we can do more."

I had been to the State Finals twice, losing both times in the afternoon. I did not want just to go again, I wanted to stay all day and win it.

THE QUEST

We knew what to expect the week before the finals. It would be a carnival-like atmosphere filled with interviews, photographs and phone calls. Players were observed, analyzed, categorized. It helped that Coach Bush and I had been there before.

About 2,000 tickets remained, but Gene Cato, commissioner of the Indiana High School Athletic Association expected them to be sold quickly. He was correct. Within 104 hours all

41,046 tickets had been sold, the most ever for any high school game.

Concord and Anderson would meet in the first game, Southport and BNL in the second. I do not think we ever talked about whether we would rather face Concord or Anderson at night. It would be immaterial if we did not defeat the Cardinals. Concord did defeat Anderson, 70-66.

* * *

It looked for a time as if it would not matter who had won that first game. Led by southpaw William Moore, Southport went on a scoring spree and we trailed big time, 32-18, midway through the second quarter. Moore had scored 23 of those 32 points.

It may have appeared to some that we were out of chances, our final opportunity for a title nearing an end. That changed quickly. Dwayne Curry buried a trey and we had cut the deficit to 32-23 at the half.

During the intermission Coach Bush did a great, great job—maybe the best coaching he did the whole time I was at BNL. He made adjustments about how we were going to defend people, what we needed to do offensively. He ordered 5-9 Curry to guard the rugged 6-2 Moore, an assignment one writer said was like ordering a gnat to molest an elephant.

The coach said we were playing tentatively, needed to be more aggressive. "If you are going to get beat," he said, "let's go down fighting."

Defeat was not a word we wanted to hear. Curry stuck to Moore like flypaper, holding him to 1 of 11 field goal attempts in the second half. Dwayne stuck his nose in there, tormenting Moore with his quickness. That was the kind of players we had. They enjoyed challenges. If the coach told them to do something, that is what they did.

The offense was much sharper, too. Bush hit a jump shot as the third quarter expired. We had erased the deficit and led 43-39.

We would not score another field goal. We did hit 15 of 17 free throws and held on to win 58-55. It was another game we were fortunate to win.

There was little celebration. Within minutes we were on our way back to our rooms at the Airport Hilton. In a few short hours we would face the Concord Minutemen for the state championship. That dream was now within reach.

We were supposed to rest, sleep if we could. The anticipation, as it always is before a big game, was too overpowering. We laid in bed, eyes open in stillness. We all seemed more relaxed than nervous. Fear was never a problem. We were never scared of any team we played.

We had the attitude that it would take an extraordinary effort to beat us. The two teams that had done so during the season, Lawrence North and New Albany, had played extremely well to do it.

Darkness had fallen over the airport when we boarded the bus back to the Hoosier Dome that night. Coach Bush asked us to be in uniform earlier than usual. He wanted to explain what he had observed about Concord from video tapes.

We listened closely. This chance for a shot at the title was what we had worked for all year. This was why we had spent the summer playing. This was why we had put in all those years of effort.

Coach Bush said he was proud we had come this far, then added, "Hey! Let's not be satisfied. We did not come here just to win the afternoon game. We came to win the championship."

Before we left the dressing room, Curry reminded us, "Don't bring anything back here with you. Leave everything you have out on the floor. Play as hard as you can. If you have to be carried off the floor, that's what we will do."

We had come too far to fall short. We did not want to return to the locker room with any regrets. We did not want to hear any "I wish I had done something different" comments.

If our best effort was not good enough so be it. If we played hard, went all out, there would be no regrets if we lost.

Both teams played well early in the game, then went into a lull before Concord picked up the pace to lead, 37-32 at the half. We erased that deficit, then played even with the Minutemen and the third quarter ended in a 46-46 deadlock.

Concord took the lead and was ahead, 58-52, with 2:38 to play. Coach Bush was concerned because Concord had good ball-handlers who would try to keep possession and protect its margin. He told the team, "Get the ball to Damon and he'll make something happen."

He would say later he had seen a gleam in my eye, a look that said I would not be denied.

After that timeout I called the players together on the floor. "We've talked about this all year. We have more than 2 minutes to make up a 6-point difference," I reminded them. The players knew where the ball needed to be and when it needed to be there. They all knew it was time for me to take control of the game.

This was the most competitive group of players I had been around. I had, perhaps, played with more competitive individuals, but not a more competitive team.

Concord seemed to sense we were coming after it with everything we had. It started missing shots. We started hitting ours.

I made two free throws, scored on a drive at 1:45, was fouled and made the free throw. We trailed, 58-57. I scored on a rebound after a missed shot with 1:15 left and we were ahead, 59-58. Jamar Johnson scored to put Concord back in the lead, 60-59.

I was fouled on the next possession, made both shots and we were in front 61-60 with 38 seconds to play. Concord missed another shot and again I was fouled. Both shots hit the mark and we led 63-60. I had scored 11 points in just over 2 minutes, but that was not on my mind.

There were 24 seconds left on the clock, an eternity, especially when a 3-point shot can tie the score. Jamar Johnson fired from long range, but the ball hit the back of the rim. Jeff Massey grabbed the rebound and fired another long shot. It hit iron and caromed off to the right to Micah Sharp. He stepped behind the arc and lofted another bomb. It, too, was off target.

We preserved the 3-point victory when Jason Lambrecht seized the rebound and held on as the final horn sounded to create the jubilation which followed.

We had won the title. Our dream had come true. We were the 1990 state champions.

* * *

As soon as the players quit pounding on each other in celebration I ran into the stands to where my Mom was crying with happiness. Dad wrapped his arms around me in a bear hug and raised me into the air. I am sure he was as happy as I was.

Mom and Dad had been a big part in what I had helped accomplish. I wanted to share the excitement with them, thank them for what they had done for me and all the help they had given me over the year. They had instilled in me the drive to be able to accomplish that goal. They were the two people I wanted to share the exhilaration of the moment.

There are no others that I think any more about, that I have any stronger feelings for or who played a greater part of who I am or what I have done, than my parents.

As I have said, Dad was demanding. He expected a lot of me. As most fathers, he was reticent about revealing his true feelings.

A few days before the State Finals, Dad told me for the first time ever that he thought I was a good player. I had known that, but he had never come out and said so clearly that he was proud of what I had done and was pleased with how I had handled the attention and distractions. That was something special for me as I went into the finals. It gave me an extra drive.

At the time—and it may still be—that championship was the greatest feeling I ever have had. It was a kind of a self-satisfaction to have reached the goal we had set for ourselves and our team.

Making it even sweeter was the fact we had proved the nay sayers wrong. We had read all year about BNL having been there, had never won, that BNL could not do this, would never win it all. We had been told we—an assortment of country kids—could never compete against big city schools.

Those skeptics gave us an incentive to work harder. We had proved them wrong, which was a great satisfaction. We had repaid our own fans who did believe in us.

We had been more successful than any team that had ever played at BNL. A lot of players had been better, a lot of teams had more talent. What separated us from the other teams was the fact these kids were winners.

* * *

I had looked forward to winning the state championship. I had not thought about the Trester Award, the prized sportsmanship plaque given each year to a senior who plays in the Final Four.

Each school nominates a candidate for the honor and I had assumed BNL officials had selected Curry. Dwayne, as I mentioned, had a 4.1 grade point index, was active in extracurricular activities at school, was a student leader, the son of a minister, a top-flight kid with a great attitude. That is why I was surprised when it was announced that I had won the award.

Shannon Cummings had won a similar award at the girls State Finals, the first time the honors had gone to two people from the same school.

* * *

I had finished my senior season with 972 points, 31.4 per game. I was just as proud of the 211 assists I had that year, almost 100 more than I had in any previous season. I also had 292 rebounds, the most of my career. Those assists and rebounds, I think, showed that I had been a complete player, not just a scorer.

In my four years I had averaged 28.4 for a total of 3,134 points. I had pulled down 969 rebounds, an average of 8.8 per game, and handed out 551 assists, a 6.9 average in those 110 games.

Those statistics were nice, but I was much happier that I had—like this 1989-90 team—been a winner. Our teams, under Coach Bush, had won 99 of 110 games.

* * *

Back in the locker room the players put Coach Bush and his assistants, Mark Mathews and Dave Abels, under the showers. Their suitcases had to be brought from the bus so they would have dry clothes to wear home.

The place was a den of noise as it should be. Four weeks earlier, 4,200 players had begun the tournament with dreams of a state championship. The 12 of us were the only ones whose dream had come true.

It was well past midnight when the BNL cruiser reached Bedford. The downtown area was filled with cars, parked so close, one person said, "You could walk around the square on top of them." The occupants were there to see the team that had brought the community a state championship.

The next day, at least 5,000 fans were at the BNL Fieldhouse. They came in Sunday suits, bib overalls, and BNL sweatshirts to honor the players and coaches. They enjoyed this date with destiny, this special moment in time, as much as we did.

My parents, who had shunned the limelight for four years, joined us on the platform when principal Steven Sailor, talking about me, said, "He is the kind of young man who will never come through these doors again."

I appreciated that. There will, however, always be young men and women who, too, can live dreams if they work hard, dedicate themselves to a cause, set goals and have parents willing to make sacrifices.

* * *

That state championship will always remain one of the greatest thrills of my basketball career. After we were defeated in the earlier State Finals by Marion and Muncie Central, some fans said we would never win a title. It is always good to prove skeptics wrong.

PART IX

COACH DAN BUSH

Coach Bush, still "Danny" to fans who watched him play at Oolitic and later at Indiana State, is one of the most important people in my life.

He and Dad played independent basketball for a number of years so I have known him since I was a toddler.

We went through a lot together. He coached a lot of players, but I was the only one he had for four years. He was always there if I needed advice or someone to listen.

I stood behind Coach Bush, never questioned his authority. It really does not matter what a player wants or what someone else may want for him, it is what the coach wants that is important. If a coach wants a player to score points, he should try to score points, if the coach wants a player to do something else, he should try to do that. It is the coach who decides who will play and how much he will play.

Coach Bush and I are a lot alike. No one detests losing any more than he and I. I hate to lose, he hates to lose. It eats him up, it eats me up.

I took a lot of the 11 losses we had at BNL personally, and I'm sure Coach Bush did, too. I thought at times we might have won if I had done something differently. Chances are he replayed some of those losses and took some of the blame, too. We won so many games it is easier, as the coach often said, to remember the losses.

We had an understanding. He was the coach, I was the player. He did not have to say, "Damon, you are going to do this."

I did not have to ask, "Coach, do you want this done?" Usually we were on the same wave length, saw eye-to-eye in most cases.

A lot of things went unsaid. I knew when I did not play well. There were times he did not say anything to me because he knew that I was aware of what I did wrong or what I needed to do.

The coach gave me more responsibility each year, but I tried never to overstep the bounds he set for me.

I'm not saying he never criticized me. I was a teenager and he was the coach so that was natural. One year at Jennings County, he was all over me at the half. I mean he was on me good, probably as much as he ever had been. He told me in front of the team that I was not playing well. Chances are I was not.

We were up by a big margin and I was sitting there thinking, "Man we are up by 20. What in the world is he yelling about?" I never said anything back to him. I was probably thinking, however, that I would ask other players on the bus ride home, "What was that idiot yelling at us about?"

The coach deflected the press, screened news media requests, limited my interviews to a few reporters he knew would be fair. He was my shield against excessive distractions and I appreciated that. Our phone number at home was unlisted early in high school and it was the coach who received most of the inquiries from colleges.

It helped, too, that Dad and the coach knew each other well. Before that Bloomington game in my freshman year, Dad called Bush and said, "You should know that some people are upset about the way you are using Damon. There is something else you should know, too. I am not one of them. You are having him do some things I told him he would have to learn."

He and my Dad often kidded each other. After our loss to Muncie Central in the state finals my sophomore year, we all were downcast as could be expected. Dad came into the dressing room, saw each of us had his head down, and said, "You all played well. You have nothing to be ashamed of so go back out there with the fans. They won't shoot you." Then he looked at Coach Bush and said, "Maybe, you'd better stay in here."

Terre Haute North, the team we beat in the semistate on our way to the championship, was coached by Jim Jones. Dad jokingly told coach before that game, "We have a chance to beat North. Its coach is from Oolitic." Both Coach Bush and Jones were graduates of Oolitic High, one of the schools that formed Bedford North Lawrence.

That was the kind of relationship they had, the kind the coach and I also had to a certain degree.

I remember Coach Bush asking me about all the false rumors that floated around town when I was in high school. I had done this, done that, been here, been there—or so the stories went. I told the coach that if ever I got arrested I would tell the jailer to keep me in the cell and throw away the key. I knew if Dad ever came for me his punishment would be worse than whatever the penal system gave me.

Chances are Bush's son, Alan, felt the same way. I should point out that the coach was as tough on Alan as my Dad had been on me. It is never easy for a coach to have his own son as a player, but the coach handled the situation well. He gave Alan no favors, probably was rougher on him than any other player.

I know he received an anonymous letter in mid-season saying BNL would never win a championship with Alan on the team. He knew better, the players knew better. We realized that to win Alan would have to be a big part of the team. He would prove that throughout the season and in the tournament.

I am sure the fact that Alan proved his critics wrong and had played a major role in our championship was very satisfying to Coach Bush.

I have a lot of respect for Dan Bush. He is a great coach who understands the game and he was—and is—a joy to be around.

PART X

ALL STAR SUMMER

It was good that we were on spring vacation the week after the State Finals. I had a chance to relax on the beach in Florida for a few days. The weeks to follow would be as hectic as the basketball season had been.

Again I had been named to the all-state team, the first player ever to make that elite group for four straight years.

I also was inducted into the Gatorade Circle of Champions as the national high school player of the year. That award was made in Bedford where Mayor John Williams proclaimed "Damon Bailey Day" and gave me a limestone key to the city. That same week I received the Naismith award in Atlanta.

Within a few days, the *Indianapolis Star* informed me that I had been named Mr. Basketball by coaches and sports writers. Another of my dreams had come true. I was even happier knowing that Coach Bush had been selected to coach the all-stars and that some of my former AAU teammates also would be on the team.

I had received 331 of 348 votes cast for Mr. Basketball, which was a surprise to me. I thought that the vote might be close enough that Eric would be named co-Mr. Basketball. That would not have bothered me. I have great respect for Eric as a player and as a person.

It is difficult, however, to compare players. I can do things for a team that Eric cannot do and Eric can do things for a team that I am unable to do. It is possible to compare two point guards, but not a 6-3 forward-guard with a 7-0 center.

*My first national
AAU most valuable
player award*

*—July 30, 1983
at South Bend*

☆☆☆☆☆

*"I knew not to be too pleased with myself.
My parents would not tolerate any
smugness on my part."*

Unbeaten sixth grade team at Heltonville in 1984, Jason Cain, me, Coach Turner, Jamie Beedie and Jay Faubion

That's me dunking the ball in junior high at Barr-Reeve.

*I drive on a defender early in my
high school career.*

At Heltonville store with owner "Bonehead" Faubion

Courtney and I

Stacey and I

Courtney, Stacey, Dad,
Judy & Guy Waldo

Coach Bush gives me encouragement at
emotional high school farewell.

Surrounded by newsmen after breaking state scoring record at Seymour

Sign outside school after 1990 regional title

A yard sign near Heltonville shows fan support.

*Jimmy Jackson applies defense in an
Ohio State game.*

Me, Steve Mozingo, Troy Terrill and Elliot Hatcher after 1990 AAU Championship at St. Petersburg

"It was unbelievable how well our AAU teams played together. The cohesion, the unselfishness, the bond we formed was amazing."

Splitting the defense in Big Ten
game against Purdue

Coach Knight approves of my game in 1992 Hoosier Classic at Market Square Arena.

I acknowledge tributes at final
home game at I. U.

Courtney and I in post-game farewell at Assembly Hall

Closing out my college career against
Boston College

I pose for a picture at a 1994 public appearance.

I was delighted to be Mr. Basketball but I felt badly for Eric, because I knew he was a good player. It did not hurt our friendship. We had played together, had become friends. We realized we were two different type players and that one of us was not better than the other.

The Mr. Basketball title meant I had swept the "Triple Crown" by also playing on the state championship team and winning the Trester Award. No one had done that except Dave Colescott of Marion in 1976 and Bob Plump of Milan in 1954. That also was about the time I was named a McDonald's all-American.

All that recognition in such a short time gave me a lot of satisfaction. All the years of practice, all the hours of effort, all the sacrifices, all the miles I had run before school, all the hours in the gym at Heltonville had paid off.

I had done those things in hopes of winning a state championship for my team and being recruited to play at I.U. I had realized both dreams.

Within a few months I would have to prove myself again. Those awards and press clippings would mean nothing to Bob Knight when practice started in October at I.U.

It would not be a case of what I had done, but what I could do. In basketball you must earn the right to compete at each level to which you advance. Nothing is a given. It would not matter to Coach Knight if I had been the greatest scorer in Indiana basketball. All he would care about would be what I could do for the team.

NBA teams would not care if I played at Indiana, was the fifth, six or seventh all-time scorer. What matters is not what I had done yesterday, but what I can do tomorrow.

Once I retire I can look back and say I had a good career, set scoring marks, won a high school championship. That spring of 1990, I did not have time to relax and bask in the glory of what I had done.

I think we all should strive to create as many memories as we can. Once we are through playing or are finished with whatever we do, we can sit back with our grandkids and reflect on those memories. Life is short so we need to accomplish as much as we can in the time we have.

* * *

A teenager, to be a complete individual, cannot spend all his hours in the gym, cannot let the game of basketball dominate his life.

I was in the choir all four years in high school. We had a little swing group, about seven girls and seven boys, including some other players from the basketball team, that performed with the choir. We did skits, danced and sang for service clubs and other groups. When I was a senior, we redid "Dueling Banjos" into a skit we called "Dueling Basketballs." We had a lot of fun.

Throughout high school I continued to date Stacey, who was one of the BNL cheerleaders. All the attention I received bothered her, but she seldom complained. We did not go out often, preferring to be at her house, my parents' home or with friends.

My studies were important to me as they should be to any athlete. An athlete cannot participate in sports forever; he needs to be prepared for the time when he no longer can compete at a higher level or becomes too old to do so. As I recall I had a 3.7 grade point index. I ranked in the top 10 percent in a graduating class of 378 and scored 1010 on the SAT.

The four years had passed quickly. It seemed only a short time ago that I had entered BNL as a freshman.

* * *

That summer seemed to bring another basketball game each week. I really do not enjoy all-star games; they are not for me. I am not a one-on-one type player, not that I could not be if asked. That is just not the way I do things because I am more of a team player.

All-star coaches try to make the contests team games, but to do so is very hard. You do not really practice, you just go out and play. I like to work to get other players open, then get them the ball. I expect them to help get me free and to get me the ball.

Most all-star players want to score, to become the focus of attention.

The McDonald's all-American game at Market Square Arena was a typical all-star game. So was the Derby Festival Classic game at Louisville as were the two Team Indiana-Soviet National games. I did play well against the Soviets in one game, not so well in the other.

The two Indiana-Kentucky games were somewhat different. Coach Bush had more time to mold us into a team and six of us - Montross, Matt Waddell, Linc Darner and the Ross twins, Joe and Jon, had played together for years on the AAU team.

Our Indiana team came from behind to defeat Kentucky at Freedom Hall in Louisville in the first of the two-game set. Montross played well, scoring 20 points and owning the boards with 17 rebounds. I scored 24 and had four assists in the 94-90 overtime victory.

The second game was just as close. Indiana won, 83-82, at Market Square in Indianapolis. Jamar Johnson, who had played well for Concord in the State Finals, led the Hoosier team with 22 points. I had 13 points and was credited with blocking a shot that would have won the game for Kentucky.

We had given Coach Bush two more victories to remember.

In July, I joined Montross, Jimmy Jackson of Ohio State, Arriel McDonald of Minnesota and other players on the North squad, at the U.S. Olympic Festival in Minneapolis.

We lost the championship to the South, 121-120, in what was my best game of the festival. I hit all five 3-point shots that I took and scored 25 points.

Jackson, who now plays for Dallas in the NBA, and I became close friends while at the festival. He razzed me about how Ohio State would beat us during the season, but he also taught me a lot about Big Ten basketball. He is a great player; a nice person.

In late July, Montross and I teamed up for our last AAU tournament at St. Petersburg. The Municipal Gardens team also included Alan Henderson and Brian Evans, both of whom would eventually play at I.U. We won another Amateur Athletic Union title, defeating a Detroit team, a great squad from Memphis, and Team Florida, 98-77, in the finale. I made the all-tournament team and Montross won his first AAU most valuable player award.

That AAU group had a lot of talent, but certainly not the most of any team in the tournament. The Memphis team, for example, had Anfernee Hardaway, now an NBA all-star, Randy Carter, who played at Minnesota, and Corey Beck from the 1994 Arkansas NCAA championship team. Other NBA players in the tournament were Rodney Rogers, Wake Forest, Chris Webber, Michigan, and Clifford Rozier, Louisville.

Summer basketball was over. It was time to think about my next four years with Bob Knight.

PART XI

THE FRESHMAN

I had talked with Pat Knight, the coach's son, at the Team Indiana-Soviet game at Assembly Hall. He mentioned that he did not have a roommate for his freshman year at I.U. so I invited him to share the house Richard Wright, my long-time friend from BNL, and I had rented. Pat's friend Joe Scifres, who also was from Bloomington, joined us, too.

Bloomington, I would soon learn, was a bigger rumor mill than Bedford. I heard stories that Coach Knight had asked me to room with Patrick, hoping he might adapt to my more conservative life style.

That was scuttlebutt, untrue. The coach never mentioned it, never suggested his son move in with us. Patrick has his own personality, his own interests, and I do not think any characteristics I had would have rubbed off on him.

Patrick is a lot of fun and there is never a dull moment when he is around. He would make my freshman year interesting.

College, especially that first year, would be a big adjustment for me as it is for every student. I was away from home, Mom and Dad were not there anymore to make sure I did my homework or to tell me to be home at a certain time. College takes a lot of self-discipline.

Like any other kid I may have made some mistakes—none of which were serious—my freshman year. I lived with that, learned from it and moved on.

After that freshman year, Richard and I rented an apartment, as did Patrick and Joey. We decided that four students in one house resulted in too many visitors and too much traffic. We should have had a revolving door, so many people came and went.

Patrick and I continued to be friends. We still are today.

*   *   *

Coach Knight never suggested a course of study for me. The team has an academic counselor who works with the players. Knight does not care what major a player pursues as long as it leads to a career after basketball. And he does not get involved in academic endeavors as long as the player goes to class and makes his grades. He will not tolerate absenteeism or poor class work. I had been a good student at Bedford North Lawrence and had no problem adapting to a college curriculum.

*   *   *

I had been too busy that summer to spend much time in Bloomington practicing with the returning players who had remained on campus. School had begun before I started working out with the upperclassmen: Lyndon Jones, Eric Anderson, Jamal Meeks, Calbert Cheaney, Matt Nover, Chris Reynolds, Greg Graham, Pat Graham, Todd Leary and Chris Lawson.

Lawrence Funderburke, who had left the team as a freshman, had asked Coach Knight to return. College basketball is not a democratic institution, but Knight allowed his players to vote on the matter. The team decided against Lawrence's return and the coach accepted that decision.

Pat Knight and I, the only freshmen on the team, did not vote. We had not been there the previous season and did not know the circumstances involved.

*   *   *

I not only would be wearing a new uniform, I would be wearing a new number. Anderson already had the No. 32 I had worn in high school so I chose No. 22 as my I.U. number.

I had not seen Coach Knight that summer and really had not that much contact with him, even though he had been to a lot of our BNL games over my four years. I knew he demanded a lot from his players, was relentless in his pursuit of excellence, and had an offense that was much more complex than what any high school had.

I would learn a lot more about him in the four years to come.

* * *

No one ever forgets the first practice with Coach Knight. I certainly will not. It seemed to last forever, maybe no more than three hours, but it seemed like an eternity. No high school practice ever had been that hard.

I was playing against kids—men, actually—who were bigger and better and quicker than anyone I had played against in high school. To have a practice that intense the first day against some of the best basketball players in America was tough.

I do not think I ever had been so tired in my life. I went home and "died" after that workout. So did Patrick, who had been around those practices since he was knee-high to a grasshopper. It was a new experience, but one to which I would become accustomed.

Practices continued to be hard and long through the remainder of October and into November.

It was a difficult time, but the older players said, "Hang on until the coaches clinic. The practices usually ease up after that." The clinic, I learned, was a session Knight conducted for visiting coaches, two or three weeks into practice. The players run through drills while coach explains what we are doing.

The clinic was sort of a turning point. I cannot say practices became easier, but they did not seem to be as intense. Over the next three years I would look forward to those clinics, knowing practices were about to be shorter and that longer scrimmages and fewer drills were ahead.

Practices were taped and the tapes were at times critiqued. I am sure the coaches watched those tapes to see how individuals were doing, to determine who needed to work on particular facets of his game.

If I had a bad practice, I might be called in to view my effort. If the entire team had not practiced well, we all would watch those tapes.

Coach Knight, depending on how angry he was, might go over some of the film with a player or with the entire team. Usually, the assistant coaches did that.

I never felt intimidated by Coach Knight. He is going to yell. He is going to scream. He is going to swear. All that is a given. I knew that before going there. A player who goes there today should know that, too.

He is not going to hit you. He will get in your face. Sooner or later—usually sooner—he will get angry enough to kick you or the entire team out of practice.

Coach Knight does not hide what he does. He does not hesitate to criticize a player in front of the team in practice or before 17,000 fans at I.U. or 40,000 anti-Hoosiers in a dome away from home.

I do not know how it is at Kentucky, how Rick Pitino is. I do not know how it is at Purdue. I do not know how Gene Keady is. I do not know how Dean Smith is at North Carolina. I expect, just guessing, that they have their moments, too.

Indiana may be a bit more open, less likely to hide what goes on. There is nothing that happens at I.U., either in practice or at a game, that the world will not hear about.

A player, as I said, knows that going in. He has to learn, somehow, to accept it and find a way to learn from it.

If I saw Coach Knight on campus or around town I would speak to him. If he returned my greeting, great. If he did not, it did not bother me. I was never intimidated. However—and this is a big however—that does not mean I did not get really aggravated with him at times.

I detected quickly how difficult the complex I.U. motion offense is to grasp. It takes time for a player to learn what he needs to do in certain situations. No matter how good a player may be as a freshman, he will struggle with the system. It is something a player has to learn for himself.

Coach Knight is not going to tell you to set a pick there and come off it here. You have to read what the defense gives you. This takes time if you have not done it in high school. Few, if any, players have.

I did not have a hard time understanding my role. It did take me a while to learn the offense. I do not think anyone ever learns the system to its fullest extent, even if he is there four or even five years. It just takes time.

* * *

Once again there was a big buildup before the season started. "The Damon Era," some newspapers called it. I was expected to take I.U. to greater heights and I had yet to play a single game. It may have been the first time Coach Knight had been overshadowed by an 18-year-old freshman.

I knew I would not be the scorer I had been in high school. Cheaney and Anderson, both of whom could shoot the ball, were at forwards. I would have to get them open, then get them the ball so they could score. I was told to shoot when I was open, which I did for 33 points in pre-season games against Athletes in Action and the Soviet Union national team.

I could not have asked for a better place to start the first regular game of my college career. We flew to Hawaii for the Maui Classic and defeated Northeastern, 100-78.

It did not take me long to learn what it was like to play at Indiana. Our next opponent was Santa Clara, a team that was not considered to be in the same class as a Big Ten opponent. We struggled to a hard-earned 73-69 victory.

I learned then that the "Indiana" on my shirt meant every team we played would be up for the game, hoping for an upset. We would get every opponent's best effort for we were the Hoosiers, the bearers of the legacy of five NCAA championships.

That tournament also taught me how talented NCAA Division I players are. We played Syracuse and its star, Billy Owens, now of the NBA, and lost, 77-74.

In those three games I had scored 27 points and was credited with 17 assists. I was satisfied. I am not sure the coach was because I learned he would let me know when he was disgusted with my play, not when he thought I had done something well.

* * *

I learned in those tournament games that the college game is 10 times more physical than what I had encountered in high school. Players do not go to extremes to beat on each other in high school and, if they do, the referees will call fouls closely.

In college a player cannot make a cut through the lane without being bumped or hit. He cannot always move to a point on the court he wants to go because the defense will take away any advantage. If he tries to move off a screen he will be held or at least grasped. It is just part of the game.

I point this out to illustrate that just because a player is great at one level does not mean he will be successful at another. He can only advance from one level to another through dedication and determination.

* * *

Back in Indiana, we traveled to South Bend and defeated the Irish, 70-67. I scored 9 points, hitting 4 of 5 shots, before fouling out.

I did not play well, did not play long, when we defeated Louisville, 72-52, at the Hoosier Dome. I was tentative. I was not cutting hard, not knowing exactly where I was to go on the court. There were times I made the wrong cut and ended up at a spot occupied by a teammate. It was something I would need to work on.

Coach Knight probably is not as rough on freshmen as he is on upperclassmen. If a player goofs early his first year, Coach understands that is a freshman mistake. It is not wise, however, to continue to make those same mental mistakes.

There would be practice sessions and games when he was upset with me, but overall he was not on me too much as a freshman. We reviewed games when I did not play particularly well. He pointed out mistakes and let me know those were things I would need to correct soon.

Soon, I learned, did not mean next year. I also learned that once my indoctrination was over, he would not be so lenient.

I did play well in the next game at Vanderbilt. Cheaney cut his chin in that game and, as I recall, I scored all my 13 points in the 5-minute span when Calbert was in the locker room getting the cut stitched. We won the game, 84-73.

I appreciated a comment by Eddie Fogler, the Vanderbilt coach. He expressed in words the kind of player I wanted to be: "The more you see Damon Bailey, the better he gets. You don't appreciate him the first time. Every time you see him he does something else you didn't know he could do."

We did not open our home season until mid-December. We defeated Niagara, 101-64, and San Diego, 91-64, in the Hoosier Classic. I scored 14 a few nights later when we defeated Western Michigan, 97-68. Students were on Christmas break and it appeared hundreds of fans from Bedford and Heltonville were in the stands, taking advantage of the seats that were available.

That victory set up our home game against rival Kentucky and a renewal of my friendly rivalry with Richie Farmer, a Mr. Basketball in the Bluegrass State.

It was my best game to that point. We defeated the Wildcats, 87-84, a game in which I penetrated well, scored 16 points and had five assists.

My scoring dipped to 5 points in an 87-76 victory at Iowa State. I had yet to shoot more than nine times in a game. I did take 13 shots against Marshall in the Hoosier Classic for 15 points, then shot only five times for 5 points against Ohio in a 102-64 victory.

* * *

Our pre-Big Ten season had ended. We were 12-1. I was averaging 9.5 points a game and felt I was helping the team win. Critics who expected me to score 20 points a game may have been disappointed. I had to please Coach Knight, not them.

By then Coach Knight was on me for not playing hard. I thought I had been, but he disagreed. And he may have been correct.

He seemed happy with the decisions I made on the court, was pleased with my fundamentals and knowledge of the game and did not criticize my shooting, passing, dribbling or ball handling. Those things were not the problem.

My problem as he saw it was that I did not play hard all the time. Whether I did or did not, I do not know. I suppose everyone can play harder than he or she does. I do not know that you really ever play as hard as you can.

He would tell me about it. He would tell the assistant coaches about it. He would tell reporters about it. His complaints about playing hard all the time would continue through my entire four years. "All the time" was what he stressed. He knew I played hard, he just wanted me to do it every second I was on the floor or at practice.

I hate to think about how much film I watched at I.U. I had so many meetings with coaches, watched so much film and was told I had not played hard more times than I care to remember.

The coaches could take any game—for any player—and make it look like he had played extremely hard. Another segment could make it appear that he had not played hard.

I think a lot of my problem, as Knight saw it, went back to my high school career. I then had to pace myself, somewhat, because I was expected to do a lot of things.

No player, no matter how good he is or how conditioned he is, can play as hard as he can for 32 minutes in high school or 40 minutes in college. You have to have some breaks. I had done that for four years, so I am sure I continued to do that at times at Indiana.

When I started getting tired I might pace myself for a minute or two, then resume full speed like I had done in high school. I think that is what drove the coach nuts.

* * *

I got off to a good start in the Big Ten, scoring 14 against Illinois and 17 against Northwestern. We won both by big margins. My freshman year, however, would be a series of peaks and valleys. I took only three shots against Purdue, did not make a field goal, and hit one of two free throws. I did make some contribution toward the 65-62 victory with five assists. I bounced back with a much better game at Iowa, scoring 11 points and again adding five assists in a 99-79 victory.

Our next game was against Ohio and I was pumped up knowing I would be matched with Jimmy Jackson, who had become my friend that summer. Ohio State won, 93-85, as Jackson said it would. It was my best outing of the season, 16 points and a third-straight five assists game, but personal results are little consolation in defeat.

I was, however, pleased when OSU coach Randy Ayers compared me with Jimmy. "Damon reminds me a lot of Jackson with his poise. He wants the ball at key times in the game. You've got to love a player like that."

Despite that Big Ten defeat, the team was playing well and I felt good about our season. That was about to change.

PART XII

MY SISTER COURTNEY

When we traveled to Michigan a few days later I had a deep thigh bruise. I thought I could play, but I was held out of the game which I.U. won, 70-60. I had not told my parents about my injury.

When we returned to Assembly Hall, I was surprised to see Dad there. It was January, it was cold and it was midnight or later. He never had been there before, did not hang around after games as some parents did. I did not know what to think.

I did not know if Dad was angry because I had not played; had no clue what to think. I went with the team into the locker room and we waited, as usual, for the coach to come in.

Dad came in first, his face showing concern, and asked me to join him. I had no idea what he was about to tell me. I knew my sister Courtney had not been feeling well, that she often seemed to be tired, but we thought it might be the flu or a lingering cold. She had not made the trip to Maui because she had not felt well.

I read the seriousness in Dad's eyes as he spoke. "Damon, your sister is very sick. She has leukemia." I had heard of leukemia but I did not really know what it was. I did know it was not good.

Athletes, as well as most individuals in strong, healthy families, assume they are immune to illnesses that affect others. We sometimes do not have a concept of what the world is like as far as others are concerned. We think those things happen to other people, not us.

After Dad explained the implications of the disease I started crying. I wanted to be alone, wanted to make some sense of why this would happen to a normally healthy high school freshman with a chance to be a good basketball player herself. I walked the halls of Assembly Hall, tears blurring my vision for I don't know how long, time standing still, the future uncertain.

When I returned to the locker room area, Coach put an arm around me and said, "I think I know what you are going through." I did not know until later that Knight had lost his father to leukemia.

Coach Knight was extremely supportive. He was very good to me in the period that followed. I do not think I missed a practice, but he did say I could skip one when necessary, explaining the team would work around my absence.

Courtney was in an Indianapolis hospital by then. Dad took me back to my house in Bloomington, said he would pick me up the next day on the way to visit her. I cried all that night and likely was still crying when Dad and Mom arrived the next day.

It was not a good feeling, never is, to see a relative in a hospital bed, sick, the diagnosis uncertain. It made me appreciate what I had. Stomach aches, thigh bruises, broken bones, no longer seemed painful when I realized someone I loved was going through something much worse. It was a reality call.

When I visited her that day she was tired and under medication. That did not stop her from looking up and telling me, "I'll beat this."

From that point on I tried to be as strong as possible, to be optimistic, especially when I was with her. Her strong attitude, I think, comes from our parents. It was part of the toughness we acquired from them. It will take a great effort to beat either of us.

I visited Courtney every day for a time, then went to the hospital two or three times a week. When I did not go, I checked on her condition, kept in touch with my parents. Once she went home, I called every day and drove down to see her as often as I could.

I am very family oriented. I still try to visit my parents at least once a week, have dinner with them whenever I can.

Meantime Coach Knight continued to check on Courtney and made sure she had the best doctors and best treatment available. His wife visited Courtney at the hospital and a few times after she returned home.

It may be difficult for those born into big families to realize how two siblings can become so close. Courtney and I have always had a mutual bond. I know that if I ever needed anything she would do what she could. And she knows that I would do whatever I could for her in return.

Her illness allowed me to reflect on our relationship. I remembered back before she was born when I knew I wanted a baby sister. I never once considered it might be a boy. If a grandparent tried to tell me I might have a baby brother I was adamant. I would argue, "No I'm not, I am going to have a sister."

Of course, we argued as do all brothers and sisters. As a little kid, I once got upset at Mom and Dad when they babied Courtney and did not pay me the attention they once had. I took my little chalk board and scribbled, "I hate Courtney. Courtney is a big baby." There was a five-year difference in our age, so I must have been six or so when I did that.

Those are the kinds of things that come to your mind when someone close to you is as sick as Courtney was.

I sincerely believe that her positive attitude played a big part in her beating the disease, at least up to this point. She had her ups and downs emotionally, but she handled it better than I probably could. It was an inspiration to see how she responded to those difficult circumstances.

She looks great, feels good, and is living the normal life of a teenager. So far she has won the fight. Of course, the leukemia could return. We pray it will not.

* * *

I am often asked how good Courtney could have been if her illness had not robbed her of a basketball career. She could have been as good as her desire would have taken her. She was fairly tall, had a lot of talent and was strong. She did not, however, want to work at it, which is not unusual. Few people want to devote the time and energy it takes to be better than good.

She did enjoy the game even though it had to be tough for her to be Damon Bailey's sister just as it had been for Sean Alford to be Steve's brother. Just being my sister, to some fans, meant she had to be great. That was a handicap for her, I am sure. It probably took away some of her fun of the game.

Nevertheless, she was good and, I believe, could have become a very good player.

* * *

I am also asked if Courtney's illness took my mind away from the game my freshman year and hurt my play. I am not positive. It is a question that is difficult to answer. I am sure it did have some effect although my statistics in the next six games do not reflect that it did. I averaged 18 points in those games, the best streak of my freshman year.

I did try to stay focused on the basketball court. In reality, however, there probably was not a time I was not thinking about her. At times I would be on the floor during the pre-game warmup and notice that neither Mom nor Dad were at the game. Naturally, I would wonder why they were missing and assume that Courtney's condition had worsened. That thought stayed with me until they arrived. If they did not show up at all, it bothered me the entire game. When that happened I could not wait for the game to end so I could call home.

I tried to keep those thoughts to a minimum. It was difficult, though, knowing the situation Courtney faced. It did not bother me nearly as much when Mom and Dad were at the games, hardly at all later when Courtney came with them.

Courtney's illness was a wake up call for me. I had learned that leukemia does not play favorites. It can hit anyone at any time.

That is why the two of us, and our parents, do as much as we can to help the Cancer Society, Red Cross and other agencies. We realize our names have been in the news, that we are recognized by people, that we may be able to get some things done other people cannot.

Our family is as guilty as any other family. We, like others, did not get involved until it happened to us. It is important that we all do what we can. Science has made great strides in the treatment of leukemia. I truly believe there will be a cure for it someday. That day is years away. Until then, scientists, doctors and hospitals need all the help they can get, be it through donations or as volunteers to the bone marrow bank. As a society we will whip it, no matter what it takes.

* * *

This may be a good time to refute another rumor that raced across the campus when I was a freshman. That story claimed my Dad had complained to Coach Knight about my lack of playing time. He never did; it is not his style. He has never interfered with any of my coaches. His appearance at the field-house that January night to tell me about Courtney had led to wrongful speculation by unknowing observers.

* * *

Coach Bush back at BNL had insisted the players say, "Thank you, sir," when a referee handed us the ball before we shot free throws. "It may not win you any favors," he said, "but it will win you some respect." It never hurts to be nice to guys in striped shirts, he reasoned.

I still said that in college until Courtney's illness. At that point she was on my mind every minute. I quit saying, "Thank you, sir," and whispered "Courtney" before each free throw. It was a little dedication to her that became a big thing for me.

Once she started getting better, I resumed saying, "Thank you, sir."

PART XIII

BETTER DAYS

After the Michigan game, we won five straight. I had a game-high 19 points, including four of four treys, in a 97-63 victory over Michigan State. I also had five rebounds and three assists.

Again I appreciated what another coach had to say. Jud Heathcote told the media, "When you watch film, you know Bailey is a cerebral player. There are not many guys who see as well as he does. His pass is always there."

That game was followed by a 21-point, six-rebound effort in a 73-57 win at Wisconsin. I again was perfect from three-point range, hitting all three shots, giving me seven straight in two games.

I mention that only to point out that shooting is not a precise art. In the three games that followed—victories over Minnesota, Northwestern and Purdue—I was 3 of 11 from beyond the three-point line. I did manage to score in double figures in each of those games by hitting 13 of 17 free throws.

To that point, the Ohio State game had been our only Big Ten defeat. The rematch came on a Sunday before a national television audience. It was difficult not to look forward to the game, especially since I would again be facing Jimmy Jackson.

It was a game when everything went right for me. Almost everything that is. I was in a zone, as I had been in high school against New Albany, for the first time in college. The shots fell, the passes were crisp, and I always seemed to be at the right place at the right time.

I was 11 of 15 from the field, including three of four three-point shots, and 7 of 10 from the foul line, for 32 points. It was the first time I thought I had played really well all season, even though I was not happy that we lost, 97-95, in double overtime.

If I had expected some praise from Coach Knight, I was wrong. I had committed a personal foul late in the game, which was probably stupid at that point even though it did not cost us the game.

That foul is what the coach pointed out after the game. It did not matter to him that I had scored 32 points. It was the mistake that concerned him. It negated everything I had done in his eyes. I would learn that the coach did not say much when a player did well, only when we did not. He wants perfection from each player each game.

Life is a series of highs and lows. Basketball can be like that. After that heartbreaker at Ohio State we returned to Assembly Hall to meet Iowa, a team we had beaten on the road by 20 points.

I am sure the fans were expecting another great shooting performance. I still do not know why, cannot recall how many minutes I played, but I was scoreless in that game against the Hawkeyes. We lost our second straight overtime, 80-79.

Of course, I did not know it at the time, but that would be the last game we would lose in Assembly Hall during my career.

As in life, tomorrow for a player is to redeem what he was unable to accomplish today. It is that way until the season, or your career, ends, even though the coach may remind you for days about your errors of the past.

I bounced back with a good game, 16 points and five assists, in a 112-79 defeat of Michigan. Michigan coach Steve Fisher called me, "An outstanding player who would continue to progress. He does what he is told."

It is wise for any player for Coach Knight to do what he is told.

That was the last time I was in double figures until the NCAA tournament. We closed out the schedule with four straight

Big Ten victories to finish 15-3 in the conference and 27-4 overall.

* * *

We were paired with Coastal Carolina in the opening round of the NCAA tournament at Freedom Hall in Louisville. The fact I.U. was expected to breeze to victory only made the underdog play harder. This was big-time basketball and a victory over the Hoosiers would mean big-time exposure.

We won, 79-69, setting up a game two nights later against Florida State. We did not pull away from the Seminoles until the second half, then went on to win, 82-60. I scored 12 points, my first double-figure game since the Michigan victory, and had five rebounds and three assists.

We had almost a week to prepare for Kansas, a big team with talent, who we would meet in the regional semifinal at Charlotte, N.C.

The first time I ever questioned why I did not start was before that Kansas game. Every player, of course, wants to start every game. This was different. I had come off a good outing against Florida State and our scouting report indicated we should use a smaller lineup. I agreed with that. The tapes of the game indicated there were weaknesses in the Kansas defense that I could exploit.

I was looking forward to starting the game. I am not sure why but I was on the bench once the game started. Kansas played well from the start, jumping to a 16-4 lead in the first 5 minutes.

I'm not sure when I entered the game, but I do recall we were down 49-27 at the half. I knew if we were going down we were going down fighting. I scored 10 points in the first 7 minutes of the second half and we managed to trim the lead from 22 to 14 points. That was about as close as we could get. The early deficit was too much to overcome and we fell, 83-65. I finished the game with 20 points and five rebounds.

I'm not saying we would have won the game had I started. Probably not. I do think I showed that I should have been in the opening lineup.

Roy Williams, the Kansas coach, called my shooting and rebounding in that game "phenomenal," and added, "I think he is a better athlete than people first evaluate him. I thought the rascal was taking over the game."

Coach Knight had been on me all year for not playing hard. When I came out of the game late, the coach met me on the sidelines and admitted I had played hard against the Jayhawks. "Next year," he said, "you will have to play hard like that in every game."

* * *

My freshman season ended. The team had finished with a 29-5 record, the most losses of any team of which I had been a member. After all, this was the Big Ten and Division I of the NCAA, not junior high or high school.

I had scored 375 points, giving me an average of more than 11 points a game.

Fans who thought I would score 20 or 25 points a game may have been disappointed. It was not a year when I needed to be a big scorer. I did not think that was my role. I had tried to get other shooters open, get them the ball. I think that is what I had been expected to do.

Conference coaches and sports writers named me the Big Ten freshman of the year. I considered that an accomplishment because there were many good first year players in the league.

* * *

As soon as we lost to Kansas I went on a weight program, then spent the summer at I.U. lifting weights and attending summer school.

I had hurt a toe before the Florida State game. It was a strange injury and we never found the problem. It only hurt when I made a cut or moved laterally.

Early in the summer I went to the Pan Am Games trials but the toe forced me to return home after a few days. As I recall, I did not play much with the other I.U. players who had remained on campus.

Softball did not bother me because I made no sudden cuts and did no jumping so there was no pain. I still played some basketball, but very little because the toe continued to hurt.

It was my misfortune to play against a softball team, which had Dan Dakich, the assistant coach, on the roster. Dan was not at the game for some reason, but one of his teammates told him that "sore-toe Bailey" was playing softball.

Dakich, being a loyal employee, told Coach Knight about my softball summer. Knight was not happy when he learned about it. He put a stop to it, or rather, team trainer Tim Garl did. I played no more softball that summer.

A player cannot do much in Bloomington without the coaching staff knowing about it.

PART XIV

PEAKS AND VALLEYS

Lyndon Jones had graduated and Chris Lawson had departed. Alan Henderson, the highly recruited player from Brebeuf, had joined the team. Anderson and Meeks were back for their final season and Cheaney, Greg Graham, Chris Reynolds and Matt Nover were experienced juniors.

Fans expected a great 1991-92 season. It did not start that way. We met UCLA in the Tipoff Classic at Springfield, Mass., and were thumped, 87-72. The coach, naturally, was not happy.

I scored 18 points. That did not please him either. He did not like my guard play or that of anyone else. He immediately changed his mind about redshirting Chris Reynolds and started testing different player combinations.

I was in and out of the starting lineup, it seemed, for weeks. I was learning that once the coach thought you had a bad game it was hard to get off the hook in practice. If I practiced well after a bad performance, he demanded to know why I had not played that well in the previous game. So, as did other players, I stayed on that hook until I played well in a game.

* * *

I believe I was a sophomore before I was kicked out of a practice for the first time. I did what players did before me and will do after me. I went to the dressing room and waited for an assistant coach to come and say I could return to practice.

It is something I knew would happen sooner or later. Everyone—with a few exceptions—is booted off the floor at some time in his I.U. career. Like others, I was so upset about being kicked off the floor that I did not play well when I returned. I probably would have been better off if I had dressed and gone home. That is not an option, however.

The number of times a player is ordered to leave the floor varies with the individuals. Some players get kicked out once or twice a year, a few may never have to leave. I think it happened to me two or three times. As a team, we all were told to leave two or three times a year.

* * *

The uncertainty about the starting lineup continued until the Christmas break. I did score in double figures against Notre Dame and in the two Indiana Classic games when we defeated Boston University and Central Michigan. I hit only one of six shots against Kentucky in the Hoosier Dome, which I am sure did not please the coach.

I was not playing a lot of minutes or remaining on the floor for extended periods.

We traveled to New York before Christmas and defeated St. John's 82-77. Again Knight was not happy with how I had played.

I did not redeem myself to his satisfaction when we defeated Texas Tech, 86-69, in the Hoosier Classic at Market Square Arena. I had 9 points and seven rebounds and he might have overlooked whatever bothered him about that game had he not remained upset about my performance at St. John's.

He summoned me to a one-on-one meeting before the Indiana State game the next night. I mentioned I was never intimidated by the coach. I did not always want to see him, however, especially when I knew he would yell at me.

It was another session in which he complained that I had not played hard. He wanted me to have more intensity, be more offensive-minded and to get a lot more things done on the floor.

He hated to see me pace myself. It took me a long time to get away from that. Maybe I never did get away from it entirely, but I was able to cut down on it.

I'm not sure whether it was Knight's talk to me or my talk to myself, but I was on the floor for 25 minutes against Indiana

State and scored 23 points. I hit 9 of 14 shots, the most I had taken all season, and we won 94-44.

If I was out of the doghouse, I did not stay out long. I took only four shots against Cincinnati for only 2 points, had but one rebound and no assists in 17 minutes in the 81-60 victory.

The team was 9-2 and ready for the Big Ten season. When we opened conference play, I was back in the starting lineup, scoring in double figures in each of six straight victories. I was as consistent in those games as I had been inconsistent earlier.

I remember the Ohio State game, specifically, for three reasons.

*It was a chance to defeat Jimmy Jackson for the first time after two losses to OSU as a freshman.

*Anderson and I had the flu. Alan Henderson was too sick to play. Coach Knight said all he could see when he walked into the room was Tylenol.

*The game marked the first return of Lawrence Funderburke to Indiana since his 1990 departure. He had become a Buckeye in the interim. He and I became engaged in a tempest that was overdramatized by fans and sportscaster Dick Vitale.

I knew Lawrence from all-star games and we had become friendly acquaintances. When I set a screen he tried to fight through it, raising an elbow that appeared to catch me square on the chin. I fell down and the referees called an intentional foul on him.

I did not think of it as something dirty. I just thought Lawrence was trying to get an advantage. Some fans did not see it that way. Lawrence caught a lot of grief. Vitale suggested that he be banned from the game for what he did. Funderburke would continue to give me cheerful static over that incident for the next two years.

When the game ended I had hit 14 of 14 free throws, including the two Funderburke created, and scored 25 points to go with six rebounds and four assists. Greg Graham also had 25.

One of the other victories was against Michigan and its "Fab Five." We ignored their press clippings and defeated the Wolverines, 89-74. I scored 22 points, hitting 6 of 10 shots from the field and 8 of 10 at the line, to go with five rebounds and five assists.

Chris Webber, one of the fabulous five, remembered our AAU rivalry. It's too bad he did not tell Coach Knight what he told the press after the game. "Damon is more than a one-dimensional player. The basic thing you have to know when you play him is that he'll work himself to death and do anything he can to win. He did that tonight."

I especially liked that "work himself to death" part.

After that game I was named Big Ten player of the week for the first time. Asked by a writer if I had become the Bailey he had been waiting to see, Coach Knight responded:

"No. He's better than this. I'm waiting to see Bailey better than this. He has improved, he has developed and he has a ways to go." No matter how well a player performs, he can always do better in Knight's opinion.

We defeated Purdue, 106-65, and were 6-0 in the Big Ten. I had averaged 18.3 points, 5.3 assists and 4.2 rebounds. A long road was ahead if we were to win the conference title.

Michigan State proved we were not invincible, defeating us by a 76-60 margin. I was scoreless, missing on five fielders and two free throws in 22 minutes. Mark Montgomery did a great defensive job on me in that game.

Fortunately, I bounced back for two good games, shooting well and scoring a total of 40 points in victories over Illinois and Iowa. I hit six of seven three-point attempts in the Iowa game and scored 26 points.

We lost again at Minnesota, 71-67, when I again did not score. Four straight victories followed. I scored in double figures in each of those games, including 24 points against a Michigan State team that had held me scoreless earlier in the season.

After a two-point game in a victory at Iowa, I was scoreless at Michigan, shooting only twice in limited action. Neither Henderson nor Cheaney shot well, either, combining for 6 of 26 attempts.

That loss at Ann Arbor, as I recall, knocked us from the top of the Big Ten.

PART XV

LOOKING FOR DAMON

I remember the day of that Michigan game well, likely will never forget it. It was March 8, 1992, one of those Sunday "made-for-television" games that started at 2:05 p.m. After we returned to Bloomington that evening, I drove to Bedford. I had a paper due for a class the next morning and I wanted to be away from the distractions of the campus.

That Monday was supposed to be a day off from practice under NCAA rules so I was looking forward to some rest once my classes were over.

I had been in Bedford for a few hours, making some progress on my paper. I am not sure of the hour but it was late at night when my roommate Richard called. "Danny Dakich is trying to locate you. The coach wants to see you," he said.

I did not want to see the coach. I told Richard to tell Dakich if he called back that he had not seen me, was not sure where I would be later or where I could be reached.

Danny is like a bulldog. It was his job to find me and he would follow coach's orders until he did. He started calling every phone number he could imagine where I might be, may have even started picking numbers at random from the phone book. He called my girl friend, Stacey, and other friends. It was getting late and he had half of Bedford up and awake and trying to reach me.

After enough people called to say Dakich had reached them, I relented. I did not want half the town up all night trying to find Damon Bailey for Dan Dakich who wanted me for Bob Knight.

I called Danny's number and asked, "What's up?"

"Coach wants to see you," he replied.

I said, "It's midnight. He wants to see me NOW?"

Dakich said, "He wanted to see you at 9 o'clock. I'll call him and tell him I found you. If he still wants to see you, I'll call you back."

A few minutes later, Dakich called again. "Coach still wants to see you. NOW!"

I said, "I still have a little more work to do on my paper, so it may be an hour before I can get there."

Danny was just happy he had found me. "Okay," he said, "I'll be on the north side of Assembly Hall waiting."

When I arrived, Danny was there, as I knew he would be. I was seething. I pulled up near Danny's car, turned off the ignition and stepped out. I was so mad I neglected to put the car in park. When I shut the door, the car rolled over the bank in front of Assembly Hall, bumped over a curb, barely steered itself between two trees and finally came to a stop down in the parking lot.

It did not hurt anything, luckily, but I had to run down there, drive it back up, put it in park and join Danny.

Danny drove me out to Knight's house where he was watching tapes of the game. We sat down and he ignored us for a few minutes. When he did come in where we were, he started pointing out things I had not done well. As I recall, we were there for an hour for a post-midnight session.

Dakich drove me back to Assembly Hall. I went to my apartment, angry, knowing I would need to be up early the next morning to attend a class with the paper that was due.

About 8 a.m. Mary Ann Davis from the coach's office called. "Coach wants to see you this morning," she said.

"Great!," I thought. It is a day off from practice and the coach wants to see me again. I had just seen him a few hours earlier. I explained about the class I had to attend, told her the coach would have to wait. She understood.

Once I turned in the paper and attended class, I returned to Assembly Hall. Coach yelled at me some more. Said I was not playing hard, da da da da da da. I spent another hour or so with him, then went to the apartment, thinking I might get some rest.

I had not been there long when Mary Ann called again. "Coach wants to see you," she said. I returned to his office. Same spiel. Apparently the longer he thought about it, the angrier he became.

We did not have another practice until the next day. As I recall, I met him either four or five times for an hour at a time in that interval.

The first time or two, I was angry, no more so, though, than any other player would have been under the circumstances. I was tired of meeting with him, hearing the same thing time after time. I think he grew tired, too, after so many confrontations.

That was the most upset I had been, or would be, during my four years at Indiana. The thought of leaving entered my mind. I was emotionally drained, physically tired, disgusted.

I called Mom and Dad. When they arrived I told them I was ready to leave, even went so far as to say, "Let's go." They said they would concur with whatever decision I made, but suggested I finish out the year on the team and the semester at school. After that, they said, I could sit down and reconsider the situation.

I knew there would be good times and bad times playing for Coach Knight. This was the worst of the bad times. I stayed on campus, however, and continued to practice.

PART XVI

ON TO MINNEAPOLIS

Despite those sessions with the coach, I was in the starting lineup when we faced Wisconsin in our last home game.

The entire team, with the exception of Matt Nover, shot poorly in that game. Cheaney, for example, was 1 of 10. I made only 2 of 6, but I still had a much more peaceful night than I had on Sunday.

Anderson and Meeks bade farewell to Hoosier fans at that game, proving it is possible to survive four years with General Knight. The final score was Indiana 66, Wisconsin 41.

We still had a chance for a tie for the Big Ten title when we played the season finale at Purdue, a team we had drilled, 105-65, at Assembly Hall.

That big defeat only made Purdue more eager to play. The Boilermakers were ready. We were not. We lost not only a share of the conference championship but any hope of a No. 1 seed in the NCAA tournament.

Coach Knight was furious after the 61-59 defeat. I had started at guard and scored 16 points but fouled out late in the game.

It did not help his disposition, or that of the players, when Craig Riley, a Purdue senior, boasted, "To ruin their championship, it just means everything. You cannot top it. This just makes my whole career. This just sums it up."

Woody Austin, a Purdue guard, added, "It is the highlight of my career. We beat them in the final game … busted their hope for a No. 1 seed and a Big Ten title."

Their remarks show what the thrill a victory over an Indiana team means to an opponent. They may have infuriated Knight, but they just make the loss hurt the players even more.

I learned later that Knight was so upset he walked the six miles home from the Bloomington Airport that evening. We were the first team he had coached to fritter away a Big Ten championship that had been in its grasp.

The next day Knight canceled the annual post-season Kiwanis banquet in Bloomington. That raised a lot of complaints, but not from the players. College students are not banquet fans.

Coach did give fans a chance to meet players and ask for autographs at Assembly Hall a few weeks later.

We finished the regular season 23 and 6, but the coaching staff indicated some changes were ahead. Knight had decided to make the NCAA tournament a new season.

He was, he said, unhappy with the leadership of seniors Anderson and Meeks. He told the players to choose new leaders for the tournament and for the season to follow. After some thought, the players sent back three names—Cheaney, Reynolds and Bailey—for Knight to consider.

Neither Meeks nor Anderson were in the starting lineup when we began our quest for the NCAA championship in the West Regional at Boise, Idaho. They had been demoted by the coach, who seemed to be looking ahead to the 1992-93 season as much as he was the 1992 tournament.

Whatever it was, the team got the message. Scoring 56 points in the first half, we rolled to an easy victory over Eastern Illinois in the opening game. Five players scored in double figures, including Anderson who came off the bench to score 13 points. I had a game-high 18 points.

That set up a game with Louisiana State and 7-1, 296-pound all-American Shaquille O'Neal. O'Neal scored 36 points, the most of any Indiana opponent that season. I.U., however, had better balance. Cheaney had 20, Henderson 19, Nover 13 and Anderson, coming off the bench again, 13. I played 28 minutes, made but one turnover and scored 9 points.

* * *

We were on our way south to Albuquerque to join Florida State, UCLA and New Mexico State for the second round. Two more victories would put us in the final four.

We had beaten Florida State by 22 points a year earlier. This, however, was a more experienced Seminole team, one with Sam Cassell, Charlie Ward, Bob Sura and Douglas Edwards. Indiana, however, had Anderson and Meeks on the bench. Anderson came in to score 24 points, many on assists from Meeks, and we won, 85-74.

That set up a rematch with UCLA, the team that had defeated us soundly in the season opener. Coach Knight seemed to be in good spirits. He had entertained photographers, waving a bullwhip in a contrived beating of a posing Cheaney. If he was still fuming from our final-game loss at Purdue he no longer was making an issue of it.

Some fans thought that season-ending loss may have been the jolt we needed. I am not sure it was. Knight did not buy the idea and I agreed with him when he said, "I don't think that losing ever helps. We certainly did not need to lose that game."

The UCLA game-day did not start well. We were going back to our rooms, after the pre-game walk through, when the elevator at the Albuquerque Hilton stuck between floors.

We were in the packed elevator at least a half hour, maybe longer, fully clothed, growing hotter and hotter by the minute. Pat Knight started to get claustrophobic and suggested we knock out the top of the elevator. Ron Felling, one of the assistant coaches who was with us, deflected our concern and took our minds off the situation. He used the time to go over the scouting report, making us even more prepared to play once we were free from our predicament.

We eventually managed to escape onto the fifth floor, knowing we had little time left to make the trip to the arena.

UCLA may have been expecting to face the Indiana squad it had beaten in November. It was in for a surprise. We had become a different team since then, different even than the one that dropped two of its last three season games.

UCLA was seeded No. 1 in the West, we were No. 2. Those rankings and that early season defeat were all the incentive we needed. We jumped to a 44-29 lead at the half and rolled to a 106-79 victory that gave us a Final Four berth.

Cheaney had a game-high 23 points and I added 22 in one of my best outings of the season, playing 21 minutes without a turnover and hitting four of five 3-point attempts.

I had spent time the previous morning working on my shot, knowing I was not putting the needed arch on it. After that session, I felt confident going into the UCLA game.

Eric Anderson had played well off the bench. I was happy when he was named to the all-tournament team, which also included Cheaney, Henderson and me, along with Tracy Murray of UCLA.

I am sure Knight was elated with the victory over UCLA. We had beaten the Bruins by 27 points after losing to them by 15 in the season opener. We were playing well as a team and we were headed for Minneapolis and the Final Four.

I had dreamed of helping Indiana win a national championship. That thought was now a real possibility. We knew, however, we would need another great effort if we were to defeat Duke.

We had tried to make the NCAA tournament a new season, wanted to make up for losing two of our last three and the conference championship.

* * *

Once the Duke game started, we were ready, taking a 39-27 lead. Duke came back strong. We went into a lapse about 5 minutes before the half, stayed that way for another 5 minutes or so. That allowed Duke to overtake our lead and win, 81-78.

Coach Knight told the team it had played well and that he did not fault it for the loss. He, however, was not pleased with how the game was officiated.

PART XVII

STAYING PUT

Even though we lost that bid for an NCAA title, I was in a much better frame of mind than I had been after those bitter, frustrating, spirit-draining hours that followed the Michigan game.

As I said, life as a player at Indiana is a roller coaster. One day you are up, the next day down.

I cannot explain fully what it is like to play for Coach Knight. It is not possible for anyone who has not spent four, maybe, five years with him to understand. It is something a person has to live. I can explain how great it is at times, how bad it is on occasions, but no one except players will ever fully understand the exhilarations of the peaks or the depressions of the valleys.

Both the good and the bad stretch to extremes. There is no better place to be when the team is winning. It is not nearly so great when the team is losing. At Indiana, however, a player knows the victories will greatly exceed the losses and that makes life bearable ... most of the time.

Our tournament success had raised my spirits. I had played well in most of the games, especially in that big victory over UCLA.

We had won 27 games, lost only seven, and I had averaged 12.4 points a game. I was voted third-team all-Big Ten. In contrast to the bad times a few weeks earlier, this was a good time to be at I.U.

I never put out any feelers to another school, although the thought of Kentucky or some other college may have entered my mind. I did hear that Coach Knight had talked with some people in Bedford, apparently in an attempt to learn if I was serious about leaving.

Looking back, I do not think I ever would have left. I think nearly every player is probably going to think about leaving at some point or another. I made up my mind I was not going to give up. I am not a quitter. I knew the next two years would not be easy. Nothing worth having in life comes without effort, sacrifice and disappointments.

I think I became a better person and a better player for having spent four years at Indiana University. I may have become a better player had I gone elsewhere. I do not know now, nor will I ever.

I am happy I went to Indiana. I am glad I chose that spring of 1992 to remain.

* * *

I need to comment on the assistant coaches, Dakich, Ron Felling and Norm Ellenberger. They do a good job of reading players. Some players do not let the coach's tirades bother them too much. They can tolerate a lot of criticism. Others can be destroyed by it.

The assistants seem to know when a player is really down. When that happens they meet with that player, talk to him without yelling and explain what Knight wants done.

In effect they say something like, "The coach gets a little crazy sometimes. Try to understand him and learn what it is he is trying to teach you. Correct what it is you are doing wrong."

This does not mean the assistants do not get on players, too. They do.

Dakich was sort of my mentor. I don't know whether it was because he liked me or the coach told him to deal with me. Danny had been a player at I.U., had been through the same thing we went through. He has seen the program as a player and as a coach so he knows the system.

He is very good at knowing what the coach wants done, although there are times, I am sure, when the assistants do not know what he wants.

I have a lot of respect for Dakich. He will be an outstanding head coach when he gets the right opportunity.

I did not know Ellenberger and Felling as well because I did not spend that much time with them.

* * *

The autograph session, which replaced the Kiwanis banquet, was a few weeks after the NCAA tournament. Each of the players was there and fans crowded into Assembly Hall with items for us to sign.

The line in front of my table remained long for hours, it seemed. It was a chance for the public to meet the players, exchange a few words, and take pictures.

Jay and Angela Michener of Zionsville handed me their infant daughter and asked their two-year-old son to pose beside me for a picture. They mentioned that his name was "Damon." I looked at their daughter and asked her name. "Bailey," they said.

Those are the kinds of fans that made it a privilege to play at Bedford North Lawrence and at Indiana University.

PART XVIII

A CONFERENCE TITLE

I spent the summer of 1992 much as I had the previous year. We lifted weights under the eyes of trainer Tim Garl and weight coach Frank Eksten.

One of them was there each day to hand us a workout sheet to follow. They kept track of our progress, made sure we did what we were scheduled to do.

I attended summer school for three or four hours a day and played with other team members at Assembly Hall in the afternoon. My schedule still allowed me to work some as a salesman on the road for Randy Hawkins at Hoosier Auto Parts in Bedford.

* * *

Each year before practice started, Coach Knight summoned me—as well as the other players—to one-on-one sessions. Those meetings were fairly general, but he continued to stress that I needed to play harder, explained what I needed to work on and reviewed what he did not think I had done well the previous year.

* * *

Practice started two weeks later than usual, moved from October 15 to November 1 by the NCAA. That would leave us only two weeks to prepare for the pre-season National Invitation Tournament.

Coach Knight, for the first time, scheduled a 12:01 a.m. opening practice, and invited fans to watch. The balconies were closed, but it appeared every seat on the main levels was filled that Sunday morning.

He did not use spotlights to introduce each player, as other coaches had done in post-midnight practices in previous years, and did not play to the crowd. It was a practice as routine as normal under the circumstances.

If fans were tired the next morning, we were even more bedraggled by the time the day was over. We returned to the hall for a Sunday morning session, and for another practice that evening.

Malcolm Sims, the only newcomer other than Brian Evans who was scheduled to play that season, quickly learned about the Indiana work ethic. Evans had been redshirted the previous season and would be competing for the first time.

We had lost only two seniors, Eric Anderson and Jamal Meeks, and Pat Graham was back from an injury after almost 20 months.

We were rated No. 4 in the nation in pre-season polls. It was a team I thought then, and still do, was the best of the four teams I played on at Indiana.

I had started all the NCAA tournament games the previous year and had played well in almost all of them. This was a new season, however, and Greg Graham and Chris Reynolds were at guard when the opening-night lineup was announced.

We opened NIT play, defeating Murray State, 103-80. I played only 15 minutes and scored 12 points. I saw 19 minutes of action in the 102-92 victory over Tulane, scoring 8 points. Sophomore Alan Henderson had a game-high 28 points.

In the NIT semifinals at Madison Square Garden, we defeated Florida State in overtime, 81-78. I came off the bench for four rebounds and six assists in 24 minutes. Calbert Cheaney had 34 points but won little praise from Knight. "Cheaney scored," he said, "but do you want me to talk about the block-outs he missed and the screens he didn't set? Cheaney scored a lot of points, but didn't play basketball very well."

Such is life, at times, for a player at Indiana.

Cheaney had another good night, scoring 36 points, when we defeated Seton Hall, 78-74, for the championship. Knight conceded, "He played a great game tonight and I use that word great sparingly."

The NIT title did not come without a price. Pat Graham again had broken his left foot in the Florida State game.

I had averaged 18.5 minutes in those four victories, had scored 23 points for a 5.7 average. I may have been disappointed, but I knew that at Indiana one extreme follows another.

I was in the starting lineup when we faced Kansas at the Hoosier Dome, played 35 minutes and scored 11 points and had three rebounds and four assists. I had only one turnover despite playing almost the entire game.

We lost, 74-69, and Knight put part of the blame on the lack of scoring from the guard positions. He was not any happier after we defeated Notre Dame, 75-70, in a game I started, played 27 minutes and scored 4 points.

When we met Austin Peay in the Indiana Classic, I was again on the bench when the game started. I came in to play 26 minutes and scored 16 points in the 107-61 victory. It was the first of six games in which I would score in double figures.

The next night, we defeated Western Michigan, 97-58, for the championship. I saw 19 minutes of action and scored 10 points.

By then the roster was down to nine players. Our only freshman, Malcolm Sims, who had been Class A player of the year in Ohio, decided to transfer to Cleveland State. He wanted a chance to play more minutes in an atmosphere that was more suited to his style of play. Pat Graham remained on the injured list and 7-foot Todd Lindeman was a redshirt.

I saw my most action up to that point when we defeated Cincinnati, 79-64, in Assembly Hall, scoring 12 points and adding five rebounds and three assists.

Greg Graham and I started at guards when we met St. John's at Assembly Hall. Coach Knight told us to use our size to post up the smaller Redmen guards. We did that and I got my first basket 10 seconds after the game started. We spurted to a

11-2 lead and Greg and I scored all 11 points. It was a night when all five starters were in double figures. Cheaney had 23, Greg and Henderson 20 each. I had 12, Matt Nover 10.

That set up our annual visit to Market Square Arena in Indianapolis for the Hoosier Classic. For some reason I never shot well there, although I had played a good game against Indiana State the previous year.

Coach Knight knew I could post up well near the basket, something I had done often in high school. When we met Butler the opening night, I was guarded by 5-8 Tim Bowens, which allowed me to take him to the basket and score.

We defeated Butler, 90-48, and won the championship, 85-65, over Colorado. I played mostly outside against Colorado, hitting four of seven three-point shots.

I scored 17 points in each game and seemed to be back in a groove. The other players saw I was hot and passed me the ball when I was open.

The media named me the most valuable player of the tournament, the first MVP honor I received in college. Henderson and Cheaney were on the all-tourney team with me.

There had been a lot written about my lack of playing time earlier in the season and, as usual, there were rumors that I might still transfer.

When I met the press after the Colorado game I explained, as I often did, that in each game I tried to do the things Knight wanted me to do: "If that is to score, then I'm going to try to score. If its to get the ball to the other guys, then that's what I'm going to try to do."

Before that trip to Indianapolis, I had spent some time with Craig Hartman, Coach Knight's administrative assistant, who critiqued the way I had been playing.

I could see on the films that I had not done some things well or played hard enough, even though it seemed like I had at the time. I needed to do in practice and games what I saw I was not doing in the film. I had tried to correct those things and played harder in the tournament.

We remained No. 4 in the Associated Press and moved our record to 11-1 with the victories over Butler and Colorado.

Greg Graham and I had started at guard for four straight games, each of us scoring in double figures each time. If we thought we were fixtures there, however, we were wrong.

Neither of us played well in an 81-78 loss to Kentucky at Freedom Hall in Louisville. We combined for just 7 points and left Travis Ford, a Kentucky guard, free to score 29.

* * *

By then I had been at Indiana more than two years and knew how the team prepared for games. We tried to approach each contest the same. It made no difference whether we were playing at home or on the road; the floor we were to play on was irrelevant.

No team is better prepared to go into a game than Indiana. The assistant coaches are excellent at scouting opponents, at breaking down what each player can do as an individual and as a team. If an opposing player does not like Diet Coke, our coaches know it. I would not be surprised if they had learned the name of both his grandmas and all of his uncles' Social Security numbers.

The coaches know what the foes can do, what they cannot do, what they likely will do. They give the Hoosier team every opportunity they can find to win each game.

For a basketball player at I.U., everything is first class. The team flies on the team plane, stays at the finest hotels, has the best accommodations available.

We had routines that we followed before each home game and each game on the road.

We practiced at mid-afternoon at Assembly Hall before road games, then flew to our destination. Once we were checked in, we met, usually in a senior's room, where the coaches went over the game plan.

After that session, the players dressed in mandatory coats and ties and dined in the hotel restaurant. The coaches almost always went out into town to one of Knight's favorite dining establishments.

Back in our rooms, we played cards or watched television until about 9:30 when the coach met with us to briefly explain what we needed to do in the game the next day or night. He did not do it in great detail, just said enough to give us something to consider overnight.

The morning before the game, we had a walk through at the opponent's gym that gave us just enough exercise to break a sweat. Back at the hotel, most players napped until a wake up call 5 hours or so before game time.

We usually had our pre-game meal—baked potatoes, pancakes, eggs, hamburger, spaghetti—about 4 hours before a game. That was followed by another pre-game walk through in one of the bigger rooms at the hotel. We watched more film, then returned to our rooms where the assistant coach, who had scouted the opponent, stopped by to see if we had any questions about our specific assignments.

The bus to the arena was always quiet. Knight was aboard and he wanted us to concentrate on the game ahead.

When we were to play at home, we practiced at Assembly Hall as usual the day before the game and had a walk through later. The day of the game Knight might call in players, individually or in groups, to talk about the next game.

As on the road, our pre-game meal, served in Assembly Hall was 4 hours before the game. The menu was the same but we did not have to wear coats and ties. At those meals, we might find a 3-by-5 card on our plates. Those cards might be a written reminder of what we all needed to do as a team to win the game. Sometimes they were for individuals, specific reminders to play hard or to be alert for something an opponent might do on offense. The cards might be just an axiom, something the coach thought would make us better prepared to play.

The usual walk through, in which we talked over the game, followed that dinner. I would then go back to the apartment, rest a bit, and return to Assembly Hall to be taped. We had to be dressed about 40 minutes before the game was to start.

At both home and away games, the assistant coaches came into the locker room and showed film of the opponent. Coach's appearances were brief. He did not go into detail about the game, knowing if we were not prepared by then it was too late.

We usually had a good idea of the starting lineup, the assumption being that it would be the five players who had been on the Red team at the last practice. If we had a game on Tuesday, for example, we knew what the lineup would be after the walk through on Monday.

* * *

That loss to Kentucky cost Knight his 600th coaching victory (at Army and Indiana), dropped us to No. 5 in the poll and plopped Greg and me on the bench once again. Knight ripped us all the way home and continued to do so the next day. He put us on the White team at the next practice, which meant we were not on what he considered the starting five.

Greg and I were angry about our demotions so we played extremely hard in practice and our White team executed perfectly. We were kicking the Red team's butt, practice after practice. We drove Knight up the wall the next few practices because we played so hard and well, something we had not done against Kentucky.

As I mentioned, it is difficult for a player to redeem himself in practice. Greg and I did not. More about that later. Neither of us started the next two games which were against Iowa and Penn State. We both sat out much of the first half of each game.

I scored 21 against Iowa, a 75-67 victory, which did give Knight his 600th career coaching triumph, then came back with 28 against Penn State, a game we won 105-57. Greg had two really good games, too, scoring 36 points.

I am not sure who had proved a point, Knight or Greg and me, but we were back in the starting lineup for our first conference road game at Michigan. My role in that game was not to score but to distribute the ball. I shot only five times, scored just 6 points, but had 10 assists and no errors in 32 minutes. Greg Graham, Henderson and Cheaney combined for 54 points and we once again defeated the "Fab Five," 76-75. Henderson, who had scored our last basket, blocked a shot by Webber at the gun to preserve the victory.

It was a game that seemed to please the coach for it was his 500th victory as an Indiana coach. "We probably played as well as we are capable," he said. He was rarely more effusive in his praise.

That was the first of three straight road games. We would need to defeat Illinois and Purdue to remain unbeaten in the Big Ten.

Cheaney scored 30 points in an 83-79 victory at Illinois and 33 when we defeated Purdue, 74-65. Brian Evans came off the bench to score 24 points. With Cheaney, Henderson and Evans scoring well, I saw my role as a passer, one who needed to get the ball to the scorers.

Cheaney, Henderson, Evans and Greg Graham all scored in double figures when we returned to Assembly Hall to defeat Ohio State, 96-69. I had 9 points and two steals.

I led the team in scoring for the first time since the Penn State game when we defeated Minnesota at home, 61-57. We were trailing, 55-53, when I fought for a defensive rebound, turned upcourt, saw no one open and went strong to the basket for a layup and was fouled. That move may have startled critics who had said my play was too tentative.

My 17 points did not assure us of victory, however. We were ahead, 58-57, but Minnesota had possession with 15 seconds to play and was holding the ball for what could be the game-winning shot. Greg Graham guarded Arriel McDonald so closely the Gopher guard was called for a 5-second dribbling violation. We got the ball back and added three free throws before time expired.

The 5-second call was one of two incidents we would be involved in that season that would result in NCAA rule changes. I would be involved in the other.

Knight did have some kind words after the game. "That's as determined as I have seen Bailey play in the three years he has been here. A real offensive key for us in the second half was his determination."

By then we had moved to the top of the national rankings.

The praise after the Minnesota game did not gain me too much time against Northwestern. I played 20 minutes as we crushed the Wildcats, 93-71, and scored only 7 points. Todd Leary and Evans came off the bench to combine for 21 points.

We traveled to Iowa for an emotional game after the death of Chris Street, an outstanding Hawkeye player who had been killed in a collision of a car and a dump truck. His No. 40 shirt was to be retired in pre-game ceremonies.

Iowa wanted to win the game for Street, one of the most popular players in Iowa history who also was well liked around the league. We managed to salvage a 73-66 victory, thanks to Cheaney's 27 points.

That set up our dramatic confrontation with Penn State in Happy Valley. We had pounded the Nittany Lions by 48 points in Bloomington. This game would not be so easy.

We had to fight—and borrow from our luck bank—to escape, 88-84, in double overtime. The drama came with 19 seconds to play in regulation. Penn State led, 68-66, and had the ball out of bounds at the Indiana end of the court. The inbound pass went to Greg Bartram, who was whistled for pushing off Reynolds, the defender, even though the film later showed Chris may have tugged Bartram's jersey a split second earlier.

Officials can only call what they see and we were happy Sam Lickliter saw only Bartram's shove. Penn State fans complained about the call for months, likely still remember it.

It was our tenth straight Big Ten victory. I played a career-high 45 minutes, missing only 5 minutes of action. Cheaney, who played the entire game, Greg Graham, Henderson and I all scored in double figures.

I did not play nearly as long against Michigan at home when we again edged the Wolverines, 93-92. The "Fab Five" all scored in double figures. Cheaney, Henderson, Nover, Greg Graham and Evans duplicated that for the Hoosiers. I apparently had not pleased Knight for I was in the game for just 20 minutes and scored only four free throws.

Reynolds started in my spot against Illinois, but I came off the bench to play 28 minutes, score 14 points and distribute five assists. We won, 93-71, and remained No. 1 in the Associated Press poll.

We were 12-0 in the conference and about to meet Purdue when Alan Henderson injured his right knee in practice, a serious injury that would ruin his season. That was the bad news. The good news was that Pat Graham had again been cleared to play.

Knight chose to go with a three-guard lineup with Nover and Cheaney. That meant at times I had to guard All-American Glenn Robinson, a 6-3 guard against a 6-9 forward.

We overcame Henderson's loss, defeating Purdue, 93-78. Greg Graham played all 40 minutes in that game and had 32 points. I had five rebounds, six assists and was credited by Knight with doing the best job of any defender against Robinson, who still scored 24 points in the game.

Fans were beginning to wonder if we could finish the Big Ten season unbeaten. They did not have long to wait. Two nights after the Sunday victory over Purdue we were at Ohio State.

We had a 70-68 lead after I hit one of two free throws with 14 seconds left to play. Jamie Skelton then sank a 3-point shot and the Buckeyes had what they were sure was a 71-70 victory. Just over 1 second, 1:4 the clock would show, remained.

Once again Reynolds was fouled on a screen. He made the first free throw, missed the second and the game went into overtime. Ohio State went on to win, 81-77. Chances are no one at Ohio State was happier with the victory than Lawrence Funderburke, who had beaten his old team for the first time.

Knight blamed the loss on our mistakes, not the fact that we had played two games in three days. We may have been tired but we had not taken advantage of the opportunities we had to win.

Any unhappiness he had with the team seemed to change to mild elation when we defeated Minnesota at Minneapolis a few days later.

Governor Arnie Carlson had protested loudly to anyone who would listen about the 5-second call that sidetracked a would-be Gopher victory in Bloomington a few weeks earlier. That had the partisan crowd of 16,638 fans in a boisterous clamor for revenge by the time the game started.

Knight scrapped his three-guard lineup. Evans, making his first start, Cheaney, Nover and the Grahams were in the lineup when the game started.

After a slow start we came back strong, breaking a 39-39 tie with 11 straight points in the second half to take a 50-39 lead. We were not threatened after that, winning 86-75. Greg Graham had 19 points, Nover 17. Despite not starting, I played 28 minutes, scored 17 points, had four rebounds and a game-high six assists.

Knight later called that victory "a great effort, one of the really memorable efforts that I've ever had a team give." It would set the stage for us to win the conference championship.

* * *

All players want to start a game, want to play as many minutes as possible. That is only natural. There is a competition within a team as there is between teams.

I was competing against Todd Leary, Pat Graham, Greg Graham and Chris Reynolds for playing time at the guard positions. Forwards compete against each other for those positions. Because of that competition and self-interest it was only normal that we might grow disgusted with one another. Practice was heated at times, but that was all part of the game. The competition made each of us better.

I do not think anyone carried a grudge. To be a team we knew we had to get along as individuals. Had we not, we would not have been winners for four years.

I had played against Pat Graham since I was a high school freshman. I had known Pat Knight for years, had roomed with him as a freshman in college, so I probably knew them better than the other players. Leary and I were fairly close and played golf together when we had time.

* * *

I was back in the starting lineup against Northwestern, the game in which Cheaney broke Steve Alford's I.U. career record, passing the 2,438 mark shortly after the game started.

Fans probably remember only one of my seven assists in that game. It is the one that came when I passed the ball to Cheaney, who hit a soft three-pointer to break the Big Ten scoring record held by Glen Rice of Michigan.

The 98-69 victory took us another step toward the conference title.

The Michigan State game was the final home game for the seniors, Nover, Cheaney, Greg Graham and Reynolds. Coach started Reynolds at guard, but I did not mind being on the bench. Players who had been there four years deserved the farewell recognition.

Greg Graham closed out his last home game with 32 points, matching his output against Purdue. He and the other seniors left the floor to huge applause. The score, Indiana 99, Michigan State 68, seemed incidental. The victory did not.

It appeared we were on our way to an easy victory later that week at Wisconsin, leading 53-31 at the half. The Badgers fought back, cutting the lead to 71-65. We managed to hold on to win, 87-80.

Greg Graham again led the Indiana scoring with 27 points. Cheaney had 22, Nover 16. I added 13, had five assists and five rebounds, but Knight, of all things, praised my defense. "I think Bailey made more defensive plays and played better defensively in this game than perhaps in any game this year."

We had won the Big Ten, won 28 games, and were atop the final Associated Press poll. We were awarded a No. 1 seed, routed through Indianapolis for the opening round at the Hoosier Dome.

* * *

Even an I.U. practice can be big in Indiana. About 25,000 fans turned out for our pre-tournament workout at the Dome on a Thursday night. We ran some, shot a few minutes, went through a few drills and were allowed to show boat briefly, which was a rare concession on Knight's part.

He, however, was in a festive mood, and wanted to pay tribute to the crowd for showing its support. To conclude the brief session, he had the players flop into horizontal positions on the floor to spell out "Thanks!" Knight was the exclamation point.

It was a gesture that delighted the fans who roared their approval. It was a good way to go into tournament play.

We routed Wright State, 97-54, in the opener. I had nine assists, the most since the Michigan game, but shot only six times and scored 4 points. Cheaney topped all scorers with 29 points.

Anyone who expected an easy victory over Xavier was wrong. The Musketeers dogged us throughout the game and trailed, 66-65, with less than a minute remaining. I hit two free throws, Cheaney sank two more, and we led 70-65.

We were ahead 71-65 when Xavier answered with a 3-point basket with 11 or 12 seconds remaining. The ball, untouched, rolled out near the free throw line. As the inbound man, I was in no hurry to retrieve it, knowing Xavier had no more timeouts and no way to stop the clock.

About 9 seconds elapsed by the time I strolled slowly out to pick up the ball, walked back to the end line and let the official count a couple of seconds off the 5 seconds I had for an inbound pass. Once the ball was in play, Cheaney was fouled, hit both free throws and we escaped an upset, 73-70.

* * *

My hesitation in retrieving the ball after that Xavier basket was just instinct. It goes back to understanding the game, knowing the rules, being able to react under pressure.

I had done the same thing, to a lesser degree, when we defeated Terre Haute North, 56-54, in the semistate my senior year in high school. When North scored with 6 seconds left I stood out of bounds until the referee counted off 4 seconds, then threw it long down court, knowing the other 2 seconds would be gone by the time anyone touched the ball.

I mentioned the 5-second guarding call Greg Graham created against Minnesota earlier. That and the incident I created in the Xavier game caused two rule changes the next year.

The 5-second call against a dribbler was eliminated. The rules committee also voted to stop the clock after every basket in the last minute of all games. Incidentally, Clem Haskins of Minnesota and Pete Gillen of Xavier, the two coaches involved in the two incidents, were members of the College Basketball Rules Committee.

* * *

Indiana and Louisville, despite championships, had never met in an NCAA tournament. That would change at the St. Louis regional the following weekend.

Alan Henderson was back in uniform, his playing time restricted by a heavy brace. Cheaney, who by then had been named the No. 1 player in America, scored 32 points and we whipped the Cardinals, 82-69. Greg Graham added 22 and Nover 15. I played 29 minutes, scored 6 points on two three-pointers.

That victory set up a game with Kansas and a victory would again send us to the Final Four. Kansas had knocked us out of the tournament two years earlier and had beaten us again at the Hoosier Dome in December.

This game, unfortunately, would be no different. Kansas led almost the entire game and we still trailed, 76-73, when the Jayhawks broke a player free for a layup. We did not recover and lost, 83-77. Our chance for a Final Four berth at New Orleans, the site of Indiana's 1987 championship, had been denied.

* * *

As I mentioned earlier, the 1992-93 team was the best of the four on which I played at Indiana. We had a 31-4 record and it had taken four solid teams that had executed well to beat us.

We had won 17 Big Ten games, second only to the great 1975 and 1976 teams that went unbeaten in conference play. We might have won the national championship that year had Henderson not been injured.

Over the three years I played with the seniors we won 87 games, lost 16.

I know some critics did not think I had a good year. Some complained about my scoring, noting that the 10.1 average was my lowest in three seasons. We had Cheaney and Greg Graham and I thought my role was to get them the ball when they were open. My career-high 144 assists for a 4.2 average indicates I had done that.

* * *

We were losing Greg Graham, Cheaney, Nover and Reynolds. Alan Henderson's knee was far from 100 percent. The leadership role had shifted to the three players who would return as seniors: Pat Graham, Leary and me.

PART XIX

LAST AND BEST

In the summer of 1993 I was selected to play on an NIT team with Bob Sura of Florida State, Lawrence Moten of Syracuse, Lou Roe of Massachusetts, Sherone Wright of Clemson and other outstanding players.

We were gone for about three weeks, traveling to Puerto Rico. then Italy. It was still an opportunity to continue to play under game conditions, which was more advantageous for me than practicing at Assembly Hall.

We did not play well after Sura was hurt and returned home and Moten left because of a family illness.

It was an enjoyable experience, but I was happy when it was over, especially because we had been away a long time and I did not care much for Italy. I had finished summer school before the trip began and I was looking forward to returning to my job with Hoosier Auto Parts for a few weeks.

I did continue to lift weights and practice with the team when I returned home. I knew the players would need to work hard in the interim before regular coach-run practices started for we would have at least three new starters on the team when the season began.

* * *

Even though three freshmen—Sherron Wilkerson, Steve Hart and Richard Mandeville—had replaced the 1993 seniors, I looked forward to my final year. I thought we had a chance to be a good team, maybe not as great as we had been in 1992-1993, but better than some people thought. We were ranked No. 19 in the pre-season poll.

Practice seemed to go well. Coach Knight, after being gone for a few days, told a pre-season luncheon crowd that Dakich reported I had been ill. "He must be sick, Dakich says, because he is practicing harder than he ever has. I just hope he doesn't get well." The man is a psychologist as well as a coach.

We thought we were ready to open the season and looked forward to it as we headed north to meet the Butler Bulldogs in Indianapolis in the opening game. We were not, it turned out, ready to play. Butler was. It was another example of an underdog rising up to bite the top dog.

We lost, 75-71. It was sickening. Butler had some good players, but it appeared we went out on the floor with an attitude, "We're Indiana. You're Butler. You lose. We win." Regardless of the reason, we did not play well, embarrassingly poor, in fact.

Travis Trice, a transfer from Purdue, hit seven 3-point shots to stun the sell-out crowd at Hinkle Fieldhouse. It was a game that would make Butler's season. It may, however, have been a loss that made us better. The coach was not at all happy with the defeat. He and I agree that a team should not need to lose a game to learn a lesson.

I was disappointed, so were the other Indiana players as they left the floor amidst the Butler fans who ran onto the floor in celebration. I scored 23 points and snatched seven rebounds but I did have some defensive lapses that allowed Butler to score. Knight did tell writers he was pleased with my effort. I was, however, a senior and I was expected to see that the team was ready to play, understood its role and knew what it was doing on the floor.

We had a week after that loss to prepare for Kentucky in a game at the Hoosier Dome. It would be one of the worst weeks of practices in my four years. We ran, we went through drills, we ran some more, resumed the drills. Knight kept us on the floor for hours it seems. It was a terrible and torturous time, the longest seven days of my life.

Coach put a lot of blame on the seniors, me, Pat Graham and Todd Leary. If an individual played poorly, it was our responsibility to see that he did not do so again. That is part of the leadership Knight expects from his seniors.

He was almost relentless that week. If we looked tired during scrimmage, he would yell, "Hey, Bailey's grabbing his shorts. He's tired. Everybody get in line. Let's run and get in shape." We would run for a while, be dead tired, then have to scrimmage some more. In a few minutes, the coach would shout, "Hey, Leary's clutching his shorts. He must be tired. Let's run some more to get in shape."

If we stood wrong, breathed hard or did anything to indicate we were tired, he would order us to run some more. It was a no-win situation, but Knight was making his point. None of us ever wanted to go through another week like that because we had not expended sufficient effort in a game.

The Dome was packed for the nationally televised game against the Wildcats. A *Sports Illustrated* writer was there as well as other representatives from across the nation. Kentucky was a heavy favorite and would have been despite our upset at Butler. We wanted to redeem ourselves, prove that the loss was a glitch in what could, otherwise, be a good season.

Knight had told a writer before the game, "There's only one way for us to win tomorrow and that's for Bailey to have a great game, which he hasn't had for us very often."

I did not know about the remark at the time, but I needed no added incentive. This was Kentucky and there was no better team, no better time, to put that Butler game to rest. Kentucky would learn it is never good to play a Knight team after a defeat.

It would be one of the better games I had in college. I was focused as I tried to be every game, but this was different. It was a game in which I was so determined to do well that I did not notice anything except the floor and the players on it. My shots fell, my passes seemed perfect, I anticipated every move my man attempted to make.

It was a game almost every player has occasionally. I do not know why it cannot be that way each time out. If I knew I would reveal the secret in a book and sell it at a premium. I suppose it is because players are human, subject to the foibles of all men. A brilliant game can sometimes be followed by an awful performance when a player's shots just do not fall, he makes a half-dozen turnovers and his man drives around him at will.

The Kentucky game was my nearly perfect game. Nearly everything went right. I scored 29 points, had six rebounds and five assists and we upset the Wildcats, 96-84. It was a game I played so hard I had to sit out from time to time with leg cramps. No Indiana fan left the Hoosier Dome unhappy that Saturday as he had at Hinkle Fieldhouse a week earlier .

Knight admitted, "That's the best I've seen Bailey play, except for spurts. This is how he was supposed to be able to play." I think it was then he realized I was determined to make my senior year a good one.

I told the media after the game that in Coach Knight's system an average player can succeed. "You don't have to be quick, you don't have to be able to jump over the backboard, you don't have to be a great shooter. But you have to give the effort. We're capable of playing with anybody in the country if we do the things Coach wants us to do. If we don't," I said, "we're going to get beat by another Butler. We've got to come out against Notre Dame Tuesday and play well again."

We did play well against the Irish, defeating them 101-82 in our first regular season game at Assembly Hall. Six of our players scored in double figures and our reserves all played several minutes. I had 14 points in 21 minutes.

Our bench continued to get playing time when we routed Tennessee Tech, 117-73, in the first game of the Indiana Classic at Assembly Hall. I played 20 minutes, hit six of seven shots from the field, five of six from the free-throw line, and had eight assists.

We won another Classic championship the next night, beating Washington State, 79-64. I had a game-high 29 points, hitting 9 of 12 fielders and all seven free throws. The media chose me as the tournament MVP, but I was just as happy about a post-game quote by Kelvin Sampson, the Washington State coach. "Bailey," he said, "is the most efficient player we've faced. He just took over the game. He sensed that when his team needed a basket, he went and got it a basket. I appreciate the way he plays."

Our next game was tougher. We defeated Eastern Kentucky, 91-80, in a game I scored 32 points and had six rebounds. Eastern Coach Mike Calhoun noted, "Bailey can shoot it and guard it. He's a leader. He is barking orders and challenges. He is tough-minded, tough-spirited."

As a senior I knew my role was to be a leader and I knew I would, in contrast to the previous season, need to be more vocal and score more for us to win.

We had won five games in a row since the Butler debacle. And now we were about to face our old nemesis Kansas on the road at Lawrence in another nationally televised game.

That game was a classic confrontation of two titans of college basketball. Kansas hit a 3-point bomb at the buzzer to beat us in an 86-83 overtime battle that neither team deserved to lose. I had a game like the one against Kentucky. I seemed to be in a zone, scoring a career-high 36 points, including three 3-point shots, and 15 of 17 free throws. The 20 field goal attempts was the most of my college career.

Not even Coach Knight was unhappy with how we played. He came into the locker room and told the team, "Good job. You got beat by a good team. You played hard. You did not give up." We appreciated the fact he had nothing negative to say after a loss in which we all had played extremely hard.

We came back to win the Hoosier Classic, defeating Texas Christian, 81-65, and 25th-ranked Western Kentucky, 65-55. I scored 24 points in each game and again was the tournament MVP. Brian Evans suffered a shoulder separation and Todd Leary went out with a knee injury in the Western game, which dampened our spirits.

* * *

I would hate to be on the I.U. team that loses the first game in either the Indiana or Hoosier Classic. That victory over Washington State was the 40th straight without defeat in the Indiana

Classic. The two victories at Market Square Arena had moved that string to a perfect 22-0.

* * *

The pre-Big Ten season was over. We were 7-2 and had, except for the Butler game, played well. I had averaged 25.6 points per game and had been touted as a potential all-American by national observers who had seen the Kentucky and Kansas games. Any frustrations of previous seasons were only distant memories.

Todd Lindeman was having some good games and freshman Sheron Wilkerson and Steve Hart proved they could play. Leary and Evans returned quickly after their injuries so we were optimistic when we opened conference play against Penn State.

After its initial year in the Big Ten, Penn State was more prepared to compete when they visited Assembly Hall. We had to battle to win, 80-72. Pat Graham and I combined for 49 points.

We went on the road to defeat Iowa, 89-75, then returned home for an 82-72 victory over Michigan, which was favored to win the Big Ten now that the "Fab Five" had matured. We were proud that we had not lost a home game in almost three years. We did not want to be the team that allowed that streak to end.

Big Ten road games, as most of those at home, are always tough. We learned that at Purdue when we lost to the Boilermakers in overtime, 83-76, despite a 10-point lead we had in the first half. Glenn Robinson scored 33 points and owned the boards.

I honestly do not recall much about that game. My stats—5 of 14 shots for 11 points, three assists—do not indicate I played well so, perhaps, that is why I do not remember it. It was my least productive game up to that point.

We moved our Big Ten record to 5-1, defeating Northwestern, 81-76, and Minnesota, 78-66, at home. The Northwestern game was a struggle.

The Wildcats, who had never won at Assembly Hall, were ahead, 76-75, with a minute left. I was posted up in heavy traffic when I got the ball, used a head fake against three Northwestern players and scored to give us a 77-76 lead and the victory. It was not as dramatic a shot, however, as Northwestern coach Ricky Byrdsong recalled. "Bailey goes over three or four of our guys and four or five of his own. He shot that one over nine people and somehow figured how to get it to go down."

I had not been shooting well and that slump continued when we lost to Illinois, 88-81, at Champaign on Super Bowl Sunday. I made but 4 of 13 shots, missing all four three-point attempts and finished with 10 points. Illinois killed us on the board, getting almost twice as many rebounds.

We needed a victory to stay in the Big Ten title chase when we faced Ohio State on the road. Things did not start well. Evans reinjured his shoulder soon after the game started and Knight was ejected for protesting a referee's decision.

We overcame an 11-point deficit for an 87-83 overtime victory to stay tied for the Big Ten lead. Pat Graham played well in that game, scoring 29 points. I had 19 and we each had six assists. Dan Dakich told writers, "It was a great effort on the part of Bailey, Graham, Henderson, Lindeman and Leary. It was a player's game."

Graham played well again when we defeated Penn State, 76-66, on the road. He scored 21 and Alan Henderson, who played all 40 minutes to prove he was fully recovered from his injury, added 19. I had a game-high six assists and 10 points.

We went on the road to Michigan for a game that would mean first place in the conference for the winner. The Wolverines were ready, we were not. Evans again was out with a separated shoulder and Lindeman did not play because an ankle injury. We were battered, 91-67. Once again I did not shoot well, hitting 5 of 17 shots for 17 points.

If we were to maintain hopes of the championship we would need to defeat Iowa at home. To do that I would have to shoot much better than I had during the mid-season slump. I scored 33 points, Evans, Henderson and Lindeman were in double figures, and we escaped, 93-91.

That was my best outing since the Kansas game, the best I had shot in weeks. I hit 14 of 19 field goals, including three

3-pointers (two within 6 seconds) and had five rebounds and four assists.

It was another game in which everything seemed to go right. Leary and Wilkerson, the guards, moved the ball well and Evans and I stuck in the shots.

Nothing is easy in the Big Ten. To stay in contention, we needed to avenge the overtime loss to Purdue earlier in the season and try to find a way to stop Robinson, its all-American.

We won the game, 82-80, but we did not stop Robinson, who still garnered 39 points. We had much better balance, however. Evans scored 21 points and Lindeman 12, including two winning free throws with 7 seconds to play. I had 25 points and five assists in 39 minutes on the court.

Northwestern again played us tough when we visited Evanston. We finally won, 81-74, in a game in which I again scored 33 points, giving me a 30.3 average for the last three games.

I did not know it at the time, but that game would have a big effect on me and the team for the remainder of the season. I tore a muscle when I fell, but finished the game despite some pain. At that point we still had a shot at the conference title.

That changed at Minnesota. We were beat up, tired and sick, the walking wounded of college basketball. My muscle was still sore and some of the other players were banged up. I scored 13 points in 14 minutes, when Knight gave me a rest for the night.

It was obvious by then that we were going to be beaten. Coach became upset at a couple of the other starters and yanked them, too, preferring to go with reserves.

The result was a humiliating 106-56 defeat, the worst Knight had endured in 23 years of coaching. He did not say much after the drubbing, realizing the sickness, the injuries and all the other problems that we had faced throughout the season had begun to wear on us.

The situation did not improve the next day at practice when I tore the muscle even worse. After that I never really practiced again. I did work out a little the day before games to get the feel of shooting, but we tried to do everything we could to let the side heal. It was an injury that took time to heal, time we did not have. I did continue to play the rest of the season, but my shooting dropped off because I had to wear a brace and could not elevate my arms.

Somehow, we managed to bounce back strong to defeat Illinois at home, 82-77. I scored 22 points, hitting all 12 free throws despite the muscle tear.

It appeared we had another victory at Ohio State, leading by 18 points in the first half. The Buckeyes came back strong, however, to win, 82-78. I played 37 minutes despite the injury and scored 16 points.

Our chances for a Big Ten title gone, we lost any hopes of a high seed in the NCAA tournament when we lost at Michigan State, 94-78. I tore the muscle again early in that game, went to the bench scoreless and did not return.

I was not about to miss the final home game of my career. We still had pride in that long Assembly Hall victory streak and we did not want to see it broken in our last game at home.

Underclassmen Evans and Henderson combined for 27 points to augment the 35 Leary and I scored and we defeated Wisconsin, 78-65. It was the 44th straight home victory for the Hoosiers, the last defeat coming back in my freshman year.

I have mentioned how prepared Indiana teams are for games. The victory over Wisconsin was a perfect example. Because of the scouting report, Lindeman, who had played well at times during the season, was able to negate 6-11 Rashard Griffith, allowing him to hit but 3 of 13 shots. Brian Evans held the Badgers' other big scorer, Michael Finley, to three baskets in 15 attempts.

Despite a protective, but restraining rubber wrap on my torn muscle, I had one of my better games, scoring 19 points to go with eight rebounds, eight assists and three steals. It was, however, a total team victory and I could not have asked for a better way to end my career in Assembly Hall.

Almost no one in the crowd of 17,000 left the gym. It was time for the annual season-ending tribute to the seniors.

PART XX

THE FAREWELL

Senior Day is always an emotional event and the 1994 farewell was no different, especially for me. I had played my entire life as a Hoosier—four years at Heltonville, two at Shawswick, four at Bedford North Lawrence and four at Indiana—and I did not know at the time where I might be when another season started.

We still had the NCAA tournament ahead, but my future as a player, in Indiana, or elsewhere had not been determined. I wanted to thank all those fans for all the support they had given me for so long. I knew that within a year, if I was drafted by a team other than the Indiana Pacers, they might be booing instead of applauding me.

This had been my finest year and it was frustrating to end the season with an injury after playing so well up to that point. I wanted to close each season, especially the final one in each step of my career, on a high note. The injury, however, was something over which I had no control. It was something I had learned to play through, do the best I could, and go on.

At the farewell, Coach Knight had some comment about each of us, Pat Graham, Leary, myself and Ross Hales, an end who joined the team after the football season ended. Coach cited Leary for his heart and the scoring boosts he gave the team; Hales for his efforts in practice, Graham for his perseverance despite injuries.

I had no idea what comments he would have about me. I probably was too busy thinking about what I would say later to grasp every word. I did hear him say, "For four years, I've probably been Bailey's greatest critic, but I also think for four years I have been his greatest fan."

I read later some of his other remarks:

"I don't think there's anybody in this building who, as an 18-year-old or a 40-year-old, has been in quite the position Damon Bailey was when he came to Indiana.

"Was he a combination of Jack Armstrong, Superman, King Kong, Magic Johnson, Larry Bird—was he a little of all these things or was he an 18-year-old kid who wanted to come to Indiana and play basketball, and play for a coach who wanted him to be all those things, I guess, all the time?"

Then he said something I really appreciated. "Maybe nobody who ever played in the Big Ten was in first place as much as Damon Bailey." That was what I was about. I considered myself a winner, even if I had to sacrifice my own scoring for the benefit of the team.

Knight mentioned the game that had just ended. "He got a tip-in, he posted, he shot from the outside, he drove, he made a half-dozen great passes for baskets. I saw him guard a guy twice ..." Knight, the needler, had stitched a bit of sarcasm into his remarks, but it was in jest and I did not mind.

He added, "He played today when most of us probably wouldn't be able to walk. We don't make a big thing out of injuries, but this kid—not just here, but I can go back to each of the other three years, when I simply said, 'Are you going to be able to play?' And he said 'Yep.' A hell of a lot of players would have said, 'Coach, I can't.' Never did he say that."

He asked, "Was Damon a guard? A forward? A center? Maybe he was a little bit of all those people (Superman, Jack Armstrong, Magic Johnson, King Kong) I mentioned. Maybe he was a little bit of guard, and a little bit of forward and a little bit of center. Maybe there really wasn't a position to put him in out here.

"What he was, was one hell of a basketball player," Knight concluded. Perhaps there is a message in what he said for all the kids who want to be basketball players. Maybe they should, as I had done, learn all the facets of the game, be able to adapt to positions and circumstances.

His comments about me that day seemed spontaneous and sincere. That is why I was surprised when I would read later what he had to say about my tenure with him.

Knight then let each of us speak. Leary and Graham mentioned how often they had gone home after practice, tired, disgusted and angry at the world. I used a slang term to explain how I felt at times after difficult practices, especially when the coach had been critical of how I had played.

A farewell is a theater of the difficult. It is not easy to say goodbye to a crowd of 17,000 that had shared my joys and disappointments. I first thanked my parents, then, wiping away a tear, asked my sister, Courtney, to join me on the floor. I really had not planned to do that. It was something I decided to do on the spur of the moment. Courtney had driven to Bloomington from Terre Haute where she had watched the BNL Stars in the morning game of the high school regional. I was happy she had chosen to do so.

Although it had been a good year for me, I had endured those injuries Coach Knight mentioned. No matter how much my knees bothered me or how bad my side hurt, I knew those aches were nothing compared to the pain, physically and emotionally, that Courtney had been through.

We met at center court, greeted each other with a hug and a kiss. "She has been an inspiration to me," I told the crowd. I knew she might be embarrassed by the attention, but it was a way to let her know how I really felt about her, the love I had for her.

She still is an inspiration to me today. It takes a strong person to pull through what she has. She had lost out on a couple of years of her life, did not go to school for a year and a half and had lost her chance to be on the 1991 Bedford North Lawrence girls state championship team as a freshman.

On that March day in 1994 I knew she had shown her determination and grit. In a few weeks she would, despite her setbacks, be among the top 10 in her graduating class. She was able to do that because of her own resolve and with the help of her tutor and a lot of teachers who volunteered their free time to see that she completed classes at home while she was ill.

That not only shows the type person Courtney is, but the quality of people in the community where we live and the teachers in the Bedford North Lawrence school system.

She was unbelievable during her illness. I wanted the Indiana fans and the thousands who were watching television to know how much I loved and cared for her.

I did not talk too long at that farewell, which was a tender moment for Todd, Pat and me as well as for the fans.

* * *

We did not have long to reflect on Senior Day. We had to prepare for the Ohio Bobcats, a talented team out of the Mid-America Conference, in the opening NCAA tournament game at Landover, Md.

The torn muscle in my side seemed to be better, at least it was not as painful, so I managed to practice the two days before the game. I did not feel I would have to score big for us to win and that turned out to be true.

Alan Henderson had a great game offensively, scoring 34 points in our 84-72 victory. Alan also had 13 rebounds. Evans had 10 rebounds and 10 points. I played 32 minutes and scored 14 points to go with four assists and six rebounds.

We had decided to play each game as if it were a one-game season. I thought that if we played as well as we could we could beat anyone.

Two days later on a Sunday afternoon, we faced the Temple Owls and Coach John Chaney's zone defense. We knew we could not stand and pass the ball around the perimeter. We would have to attack, to drive the seams one way, then kick the ball out the other way. We would need to get the zone moving with the dribble, penetrate, then get the ball in the middle to break down the defense.

We did that to defeat Temple, 67-58, a victory that moved us into regional action at Miami. Evans and Henderson combined for 20 points inside and Leary added 15 from outside. I played 29 minutes despite some early fouls and scored 8 points. My job in that game was to direct the offense, so I took only seven shots.

Boston College upset North Carolina in the other game at Landover, ending the last chance Eric Montross and I would have to face each other in college.

We had a week to prepare for Boston College, but despite that preparation we had an awful start. The Eagles had a 14-point lead early, but we came back to take a 5-point advantage with 6 minutes to go. I think that comeback showed how much heart our team had. We could not sustain that momentum, however, and Boston College went on to win, 77-68. I scored 10 points and had nine assists in my final college game.

We did not play well as a team in that loss. We had not given our best effort and I, of course, had hoped that chapter in my life would have had a happier ending.

This time I could not rush into the stands in victory to greet my parents. There were no trophies, no awards, just a pat on the head from Coach Knight and a long line of sports writers waiting with questions.

I did not mention the sore muscle in my side. I refused to ruin what had been a storybook career with an alibi. We had been defeated that afternoon by a team that deserved to win.

In reflection months later, I would realize that the disappointment of the moment would not detract from the dream I had lived. It had, indeed, been a grand trip.

PART XXI

COACH KNIGHT

Now that my career had ended I could look back with a clearer perspective of Bob Knight, the coach and the man.

There were times when I would wake up at night, hours after a game or practice, and hate him. There were times when I loved the guy. There were times I appreciated his compassion. There were times when I marveled at his insight as a coach. There were times when I seriously thought about walking out.

He can be a fun person, full of humor, witty, wise and thoughtful. He can be vulgar, abrasive, insensitive. He can be congenial, helpful, kind and considerate. There were times I did not want to answer his summons, knowing his wrath was about to be unleashed on me.

Despite these complexities, I thought that, overall, my experiences with him were good. There were occasions certainly, however, when that was not the case, like that midnight summons to his house in 1992.

One constant with Knight is his desire to win, his drive to succeed and to make those he coaches and teaches successful. A player who can endure the experience for four years will leave a winner and be successful in life. Knight does not graduate failures.

He turns teenagers into men. He makes them winners in basketball and in life. He makes them competitors, knowing life is a maze of challenges, the destination too far, the road too difficult for losers to travel.

Only competitors survive four years with the coach; those who cannot meet his demands drop out or transfer to another school. Each player who remains, withstands the pressure, accepts the criticism, will graduate a better person than when he arrived.

It is difficult to fault anyone who does what he can to make you a winner and no one does that better than Knight. He will spend countless hours searching for a way to motivate a team, defeat an opponent. He is not always successful for no one wins every game, meets every challenge. There will be a time when he may be wrong, but there will never be a time when he has not made that effort. That is what makes him successful.

No team is better prepared going into a game than Indiana. The coach and his assistants know what each of the opponents can do, cannot do, what they like to do, what they will try to do and how they will do it. They have turned scouting into an art form, detailed, definitive, leaving nothing left undone.

We were required to keep notebooks, mostly for scouting information. The coaches previewed teams and players, their characteristics, strong points, weaknesses. We recorded those details in our notebooks. We studied those notes until we knew them by heart for we were aware of the consequences if we merely scribbled them down and forgot them.

There is but one boss in Indiana University basketball and he is Bob Knight. Players learn quickly it is not their way, it is Knight's way. They are there to learn, he is there to teach. There was no back talk, no inattention, no tardiness, no disinterest.

We knew that if we did it his way we would win most of the time. We knew that if we did it our way, we would be down at the end of the bench. It was a case of doing it his way or looking for the doorway.

Knight seldom lauds a player for a great game. In his eyes there will always be something that was not done right. No one will ever play a perfect basketball game, but the coach pushes, pushes and pushes each player toward that perfection. It is hard for me to argue with that approach. It was the one my Dad used with me for all those years. I do not think Coach Knight ever said anything to me I had not heard from my Dad.

Like or dislike what Coach Knight does, he is a great coach, but he is not a coach for every player. Basketball at Indiana is not for the weak of heart, for those who fear authority, or those who avoid challenges. It takes a special kind of person to play for him, the kind who could be an Army Ranger or a commando; a survivor who can accept challenges.

There are rewards for those who can survive the situation, endure the down days. It is an honor to play for Indiana University. Playing against a Kentucky, a Kansas or a Purdue before thousands in an intense atmosphere of big-time competition is an exhilarating experience. It is a great sensation to compete against teams of that caliber. The good part is knowing that your Knight-coached team will win a lot more than it will lose.

A strong-minded, competitive player, eager to learn more about the game, probably will succeed at Indiana. Those who cannot handle criticism and verbal abuse should find another school.

The most important thing I learned from Knight is how hard it is to be good, how difficult it is to be successful at whatever you choose to do. He would be good at any career he chose to pursue. If he chose to fish, he would be the best fisherman. If he wanted to be a pro golfer, he would be the best at the game. If he wanted to be a lawyer, he would be the best of them all.

That competitiveness, that desire to be the best, is what he tries to instill in his players. If they learn that, he has proved his point. If they do not, he has tried. If it were easy to be good, everyone would be great.

* * *

I had appreciated those gracious comments Knight said about me at our final home game, and other generous remarks I read after we lost to Boston College at Miami.

That is why I was surprised to learn almost a year later that *Inside Sports* had quoted him as saying, "I got less out of Bailey than any kid I ever coached. I didn't get it done ... rarely have I felt that about a kid."

We had not talked, had not reflected on my career, after the season ended. I did consult with him later before choosing an agent prior to the National Basketball Association draft. I went to one practice that fall and chatted with him briefly. I still do not know exactly what he meant by that "got less out of" comment.

Knight is entitled to his opinion. He will say what he wants to say, even if it may hurt someone. I would not be honest if I did not admit his remarks bothered me at the time. I had given him four years of my life, done what I thought he had wanted me to do, played while injured, passed instead of shoot, sacrificed myself for the team.

After playing for someone for four years, I would hope he would have something better to say about me than that. I had helped the team win, had played in 108 Indiana victories, a figure matched only by Quinn Buckner.

Only Knight knows what he meant by his comment. I suspect he thought he had failed to make me play as hard as he thought I should. That was his opinion even though he had given me indications that he thought I had played hard and well my senior year. I did not think I played any harder, I just had better statistics.

Perhaps Knight decided—maybe after reviewing the season on film—that I had not played hard as a senior, either. I do not know. I cannot read his mind or always interpret what he says. I do know that I had to work awfully hard to get as far as I had gotten and to accomplish as much as I had.

I know a lot of fans wanted me to average 20 points a game each year. Maybe Knight wanted that, although he never said so. I was playing with good shooters and I considered it my role to get the ball to guys like Anderson, Cheaney, the Grahams and Henderson. No one, I felt, could do that as well as I could. That is why I tried to remain a team player even though it may have taken away some personal glory.

Someone on every great team must make sacrifices to win. I was willing to do that. Some fans saw the boxscores and complained that I had not scored enough. When it came my time as a senior to put points on the board, I proved that I could. Cheaney and Greg Graham had departed and I considered it my responsibility to offset that scoring loss.

It no longer bothers me what he says about me. He is Bob Knight and he will do what he wants, say what he thinks. He is no longer my coach, so I will not be offended by whatever he says.

* * *

I am often asked if I would attend Indiana had I to do it over. It is a difficult question. If I was coming out of high school now, I probably would make the same decision. Four years, however, is long enough. It is an intense place to play and coach.

Whether I would send a son there would depend on the kind of son I had. It takes a special person to play for Knight; not everyone can handle the demands. I would, No. 1, let my son make his own decision and, No. 2, I would encourage him only if I thought he could handle the situation he was getting into. If I did not think he could handle the demands, I would in no way encourage him.

If Knight called and asked me to be an assistant coach, I would at this point turn him down. I think, even if my professional career was over and I was pumping gas, I would still refuse to take the job.

I want to emphasize that I am happy with the decision I made to play at Indiana. I would, as I said, probably make the same decision again. But I would not want to spend another four years there.

It is like climbing a mountain, being in military service, bungee jumping or walking a tightrope. It was something I would do once, but I would not want to do again.

* * *

Despite Coach Knight's comment, I felt I had a successful career at Indiana. Sure, I would have liked to score more, had more assists, collected more rebounds, won more games.

The teams I was on won 108 games, lost 25, claimed a Big Ten championship, made the NCAA Final 16 all four years, went to the Final Four once. I had played in 15 NCAA tournament games, more than any Indiana player, and that means more to me than the other statistics. It means I was a winner and that was what I wanted to be from the first time I pulled on an Indiana uniform.

When my senior season ended, I was fifth (now sixth) in career points, tied for second in assists, first in the number of 3-point shots scored, seventh in free throws made. I led the team in assists and scoring my senior year, the first player to do that since Steve Alford in 1987. I was All-Big Ten as a senior, third team all-American.

I have been told that I.U. teams were in first place more during my career than in any other player's career.

Maybe I would have caught a little less static from the coach if I had tried to score as many points as I could each game. That would have been better for me individually. It would not have been as good for the team, which is what I was concerned about.

I do not point this out for self-adulation. I do so to indicate that I am proud to have been a winner and a part of what has been the tradition that is Indiana University.

PART XXII

THE FANS

One of my biggest fans has been Stacey, the cheerleader I met in the eighth grade. We started dating in October, 1987, as high school freshmen and, with a brief exception, never stopped.

She noticed my competitive nature even when I was in junior high. I began calling her after that. She thought I was pushy, that at first she did not like "that kid from Heltonville," as she referred to me to her mother. I persisted until she accepted me or I won her over.

I guess I knew even then not to accept failure or fear rejection. Stacey eventually broke up with her junior high boy friend and I split with my junior high girl friend. She continued to be a cheerleader in high school and she soon learned how much the game of basketball meant to me.

We have been through a lot together. She knew me when I was Damon Bailey nobody. We grew up together. We celebrated the victories, suffered through the defeats. Even when we were not dating as college freshmen, she continued to see Courtney through her illness.

She never complained when I wanted to play basketball. She knew I loved the game, did not question me when I played on summer weekends instead of dating her. She knew how dedicated I was to the game, never questioned me about how much time I spent at practice, did not whine about my being inattentive to her.

My dream of building a life through basketball became her dream. She realized that the game might eventually mean success for me and, consequently, for her.

Stacey attended Indiana my freshman year. She tried out for cheerleader, hurt her back and had to drop out for a semester. In the interim she started to work for a Bedford doctor and did not return to classes at I.U.

All the attention I received, especially from girls when we were out in public, bothered Stacey at first, made her "sick to her stomach," she said. The pushy kind of women, the kind who would step between us, ignore her and ask me for dates, caused her the most grief.

We seldom could go anywhere without being confronted by fans. At Kings Island, the amusement park near Cincinnati, for example, we sat down to rest briefly. Soon a long line of people had formed, expecting autographs or a few minutes of my time. We were at Las Vegas for an AAU tournament and fans sought my attention.

I know it was not easy for her, but she accepted those distractions extremely well. I will not say she always liked them, or never got angry about them, but she did learn to accept them. I tried to reassure her that she was No. 1 in my life.

I do appreciate the support she has given me. I have no greater booster. She has been a very influential part of my life. I do not tell her that often enough.

* * *

I have always appreciated the fan support that I have. That started with my family, grew at those grade school games at Heltonville and continued to expand at Shawswick, Bedford North Lawrence and Indiana.

Being mentioned in John Feinstein's book, being on the cover of *Sports Illustrated* and being on national television with the high-profile Indiana teams helped widen that recognition. So did all the AAU tournament games that took me to almost every area of the country.

Writers call me an icon, an idol, the folk hero of Indiana basketball. I do not know whether that is true or whether I deserve such attention. I do know that without fans a player is nothing. Without fans he is like a politician without votes.

It is these fans who made me a popular basketball player and brought recognition that will continue after college. They bought tickets to the games, they supported my teams, they read articles about me, they gave me all the acclaim, they bought my jerseys and pictures, opened doors to me as a businessman.

I am not sure why I have had the support I have. It may be because I am from a small town, like many of them, have simple old-fashion virtues as most of them do. I may look and act like a neighbor. I certainly do not stand out in a crowd and I am an ordinary person off the basketball court. I have never tried to be anyone except myself. I just tried to be Damon Bailey, a normal person who just happened to be a pretty good ball player.

The only times I have refused to give autographs were at Courtney's games in junior high and her freshman year before her illness. I was at the gyms to see her play and I did not want the distractions. I was her fan as she was mine.

I have been reminded on occasions that when I was in a hurry I may have denied I was Damon Bailey. That was rare and only because of the situation at the moment. That happened once when I was en route to see Courtney in the hospital. A kid at a fast food restaurant handed me the sack, then asked, "Aren't you Damon Bailey?" I think I said something like, "No, that is someone else."

Even now, I get 25 to 30 fan letters a week. I try to respond to all requests. If the writer wants an item signed and sends a return envelope I will return it with my autograph. It may take a while, but the writers will hear from me. If I am told a child is sick or facing surgery, I will try to call the home or hospital if I cannot make a personal visit.

I may do more of that than most players, not that I have more free time. I do it because I feel I owe the fans for their support all these years.

It has been suggested that the people of Bedford and the people of Indiana owe me a debt of gratitude for what I have been able to accomplish, for all the attention I have brought to my community and my state. I do not see it that way. I am the one with a debt to repay. It is I who owe a debt for the support and the recognition I have received.

There are dozens of stories about the length fans went to see our games in high school. One of my favorite incidents concerns Jay Michener, the Zionsville man who named his son Damon and his daughter Bailey. Michener, I am told, arrived home one Friday night to inform his wife they were going out to eat. "Out to eat," she would learn, was 75 miles away at Hardee's in Bedford, followed by two hours in the parking lot listening to a BNL road game over WBIW, the local radio station. The station air waves do not reach too far and Michener did not want to miss a word of the broadcast.

Hundreds of people went to great lengths to see me play. I tried to repay them by being the kind of player it was a pleasure to watch, the kind of person they could consider a friend.

* * *

The people at Heltonville have been gracious ever since I started to get recognition. They have always allowed me to be myself. They see me for what I am and nothing more, a home-town boy who just happened to excel at a sport. They have known me all my life and let me be me without a lot of fanfare.

When I go out to eat in Bedford, Bloomington, Indianapolis or almost anywhere I am asked for autographs or questioned about basketball. In Heltonville I am just Damon Bailey, Wendell and Beverly's kid who grew up out on Bartlettsville Road. I am not asked for autographs or treated like royalty.

The folks there do not point the way when someone asks where I live. They try to protect my privacy and that of my parents.

I do appreciate the marker the people at Heltonville erected in my honor at the grade school. It was a community project in which residents donated their own money and contributed more through fund-raising efforts. That makes the marker even more significant to me.

It is a thick limestone outline of the state of Indiana, a silhouette of me on one side, the accomplishments I have had in basketball on the other. The people of Heltonville are proud of it, but not as much as I am.

* * *

Once my basketball career is over, I hope the one thing fans remember about me as a player is that I was a winner. I would like to be thought of as a person who did what he had to do to help his team win, a complete player no one could call one-dimensional. I was not a great shooter, I was not great at penetrating defenses, I was not a great passer. I could, however, do all those things well, not any one thing great.

Shooters, no matter how great, can be stopped at times. A player who can do a lot of different things and do each of them well will find a way for his team to win.

So when this part of my life ends, I want to be remembered as a player who would dive for loose balls, rebound, score, maybe run an elbow into an opponent, do whatever it took to win.

* * *

Athletes sometimes are called role models. If I am considered one, I am not comfortable with the role, but I accept the responsibility that goes with it. What I try to do is instill in kids the same values my parents taught me.

I would prefer that young people have parents to use as role models. I looked up to Mom and Dad as my role models, still do today. They taught me what is wrong and what is right, taught me to respect others, work hard at what I did and that no mountain can be climbed without effort.

In my opinion, athletes, singers or entertainers should not be considered role models. It should be parents or grandparents; someone in the family should fill that role. My beliefs and values may not be the ones parents want their children to follow.

I would much rather be considered an inspiration rather than a role model. I did not have more advantages than most other young people have. My parents were not wealthy so I did not grow up with any more advantages than anyone else. I am not physically gifted or exceptionally talented. But I did have great parents who were willing to help me and saw that I worked to achieve goals.

* * *

Parents need to be supportive of what a child wants to do in life as long as it is realistic. If the child wants to be a dancer, a lawyer, a pianist or an athlete, he or she will need help and support.

Each will need to make sacrifices, dedicate a part of their lives to it. If it is a sport, the child will need to play and play and play some more. He and his parents will need to dedicate a part of their lives to it.

If it is basketball, the child should be given a chance to learn from someone who really knows the game, can teach him or her how it should be played. Slam dunks, no-look passes, between-the-leg dribbles and behind-the-back passes may be spectacular but that is not what the game is about.

He also should be given an opportunity to compete against older players. He can shoot and dribble all he wants in the driveway, but older, more advanced players will force him to learn skills in order to compete.

A youngster cannot be afraid of failure for no one can reach a higher goal if there is a fear of losing. No one goes through life without a setback and no one reaches every goal one sets for one's self. Once you lose, pick yourself up and move ahead.

Some people say it is necessary to lose in order to win. I do not believe that. I think it is best to correct your faults before they cost you a victory in basketball or in life. Do not, for example, wait until your failure to dribble to the left costs you a game, learn to do it as soon as you can.

I tell kids at my camps to set high goals, then work as hard as they can to achieve them. I stress that they may fail but they never should falter just because they did not do all that they could do to win. They can cheat their Moms and Dads, their grandparents, their teachers and their coaches. They cannot cheat themselves, for they, and only they, know whether they have done their best.

* * *

Each level in basketball, as in life, grows more difficult. When I was in the sixth grade there were at least 100 kids in my grade playing organized elementary basketball in our school system. When we reached junior high at Shawswick the number dropped to 30 or 35. By the time I was a senior, only seven of us remained on the team, which was a higher number than most teams carry from that class. Each year Indiana high school teams graduate about 1,750 seniors. Of that number, five may be recruited to play at Indiana and Purdue.

A player who makes his grade school team must keep working if he expects to remain on a team as the competition grows stronger each year.

PART XXIII

AWAITING THE DRAFT

By attending summer school as an underclassman, I was able to graduate from Indiana University in four years, something not all athletes are able to do. That, too, gave me a sense of accomplishment.

I had planned to major in history, but switched to education. If I choose, I can pursue that career if I take one more class, then spend a term as a student teacher. I doubt, however, that I would return to high school to coach. I might, however, decide later to coach in college; where I think I would be happier than at the high school level.

It takes a lot of time to make a team successful and I would be limited by how many hours I could spend with a high school team. I could not expect players to be available 3 hours a night to practice and watch film. I would want them to be, however, because I have done it for four years and probably would not be satisfied with anything less.

* * *

In those four years at Indiana, I had been scrutinized, critiqued and observed for every minute of every practice of every game. So had Pat Graham and Todd Leary. College basketball had seemed like a job in which you had to produce to stay on. It was tough and certainly not always fun for it was demanding physically and mentally.

With our college careers over, we had time to relax, at least for a couple of weeks. My abdominal muscle had healed somewhat and the three of us—Graham, Leary and I—went on a barnstorming tour of Indiana. We wanted to play basketball, once again, for the fun of it and to make some money for ourselves after years of working for someone else.

We did not have a set lineup. Former I.U. players Stew Robinson, Jamal Meeks and Mark Robinson played at times. So did Ryan Moutardier who was on our Bedford North Lawrence championship team. Indianapolis radio man Jimmy "Mad Dog" Matis even played once. Whoever showed up played.

Our opposition at the games varied. The crowds were large. We enjoyed ourselves. If we wanted to fire from the hash marks we did.

One of the games was at Floyd Central High School, Graham's alma mater. We defeated a group of former players from the school, 147-119, in a game Coach Knight would not have called basketball. There was no defense, no screening, just barnyard, dust-bowl shooting.

The demand for seats there was so great we scheduled an encore. There, as elsewhere, we sold T-shirts, autographed pictures and left with more money than what we had when we arrived. We had brought in revenue for Indiana University, it was time to bring in some for ourselves.

It was a time when basketball was as enjoyable as it once had been. There was no coach to yell at us. No one got chewed out on the bench. It really did not matter if we won or lost. The pressure was off. Basketball again was fun.

* * *

That summer I began dozens of public appearances, many at Wal-Mart stores across Indiana. That gave me a chance to meet fans and let them have an opportunity to see me off the basketball court.

It also was a chance to make some money through the sale of various items.

The crowds were huge at those events and, at times, we were unable to meet all the requests for autographs. At Madison, for example, we had to schedule a second session because about 1,000 fans were turned away the first day. School was in session the first day there and I was told absenteeism from classes was far above average.

At Evansville, about 20 disabled youngsters, each grasping a small slip of paper ripped from a notebook, arrived with a counselor. Rather than autograph those shreds of paper, we gave each of them a signed picture.

John Baker of J&J's Sports Cards, Ellettsville, who had arranged that appearance as well as the others, said the pictures pleased those kids more than a piece of gold. Incidents like that made the time and effort worthwhile.

A lady nearing 100 was brought to the Wal-Mart in Linton in a wheelchair. I gave her an autograph, a kiss on the cheek, and my gratitude for being a loyal fan. She is the type of person who keeps me wanting to play the game.

I get dozens of letters from older people, as well as younger ones with disabilities, who appreciate what I have done. If I am an inspiration to them, they are a bigger inspiration to me. It is heartwarming to hear them say they looked forward for days to watching our Indiana games on television. The comments mean more to me than all the awards and all the victories.

I never kept track, but Baker said my picture appeared on the cover of 37 magazines. Many of the fans brought those publications and other pictures to be signed.

We also used some of the autograph sessions, such as the one at College Mall in Bloomington, to raise funds for the Leukemia Foundation.

* * *

My schedule was extremely tight and I had little free time as I hurried from one town to another. My job was to please those who had hired me and to accommodate fans.

I should preface this incident by saying that the media has been important to me over the years. They have let readers and viewers know what kind of person I am. They have recorded my accomplishments and certainly they have had a role in making me a folk hero, if I am, indeed, that.

Most of my association with writers and reporters had been good. One of the few sour incidents came when the *The Indianapolis Star* reported Courtney had leukemia. We thought that was a family matter and did not want to make it a public issue at that time.

We accepted the fact when it became public, but *The Star* continued to seek information from us and from the hospital after we requested, as firmly and politely as we could, that we did not want to talk about it publicly. Under the circumstances we thought we should only have to say "No" once.

I stopped talking to *The Star* until Phil Richards, one of its sports writers whom I had learned to respect, explained that the sports department had not sought the information, another department at the paper had.

We had no more problems until I was making public appearances after graduation and prior to the National Basketball Association draft. A writer from *The Star*, knowing where I was going to be at a certain time, called my college roommate, Richard Wright, seeking an interview.

I told Richard to tell him I could not talk while I was meeting fans, that I would not be arriving early and would have to leave immediately for another appearance. I was being paid to talk with fans and store customers, not to a reporter.

I was a few minutes late when I pulled into the parking lot at Scottsburg. Almost as soon as I got out of the car, it seemed, I was confronted by a reporter who said, "I'm a reporter for *The Star*. Can I talk with you?"

I said, "No," rather emphatically. "I am not talking to you. My roommate told you on the phone I would not have time." He explained that he had driven 2 hours or whatever from Indianapolis. I replied, "I don't care how long you have driven. I told you I could not talk here. You have wasted 2 hours."

The next day the paper made a big deal out of the incident. It claimed Damon Bailey was not talking to anyone from *The Star*. I did not say I was not talking to *The Star*. I had said that I was not talking to someone who had been told I would not have time to talk at a certain time in a certain place.

I have learned later that the reporter was one of the most respected sports writers in the state. He may have been told by an editor to get the story and was trying to do his job. I was trying to do mine. I do not carry grudges or want to rehash misunderstandings, but I did want to explain my side of the situation. I have talked to *The Star* often since that incident.

* * *

I almost always tried to cooperate with reporters because I know the media are important for a player. They can make you an all-star or a no-name so I have tried to do what I could to give writers and TV and radio reporters the information they seek.

Athletes, however, do not have the time to spend an hour every day talking to the press. There were times at Indiana when I was willing to meet reporters at press conferences for as long as they wanted to ask questions. They all, however, want one-on-one interviews. I can understand that they want different angles for their stories but once I met with them individually they each asked the same questions that could have been answered at one time.

I am grateful for the press I have gotten for, as I said, the image and popularity of a player can depend on what is written and said about him. Michael Jordan is a great player, but if the press did not cover him the way it does he wouldn't seem that big.

* * *

A few weeks before the National Basketball Association draft, I chose Bill Sweek of ProServe as my agent. By that time, Ray Housel of Bedford was my accountant and financial advisor.

I had worked all my life to reach a level that would allow me to be a draft possibility. I let it be known that I would prefer to remain in Indiana as a player because my dream had been to play with the Pacers. That did not mean I would not rule out other teams that might be interested.

Although some observers thought there would be less pressure on me to play outside the state, I did not view it that way. I had lived the last eight years in the Indiana limelight and pressure had not bothered me. It would not be a problem in my eyes.

I hoped that NBA scouts would give more credence to what I had done in my senior year than what I did at the pre-draft camps. I must admit I did not play well before the NBA observers at the Desert Classic in Phoenix, shooting only 30 percent and missing all six 3-point attempts. My abdominal muscle still bothered me and because of the pain I really had not played or practiced other than the barnstorming games in which I did not exert myself.

I did better at the Chicago pre-draft camp because the injury no longer was as painful and I was able to work out before those trials started. Had I been 100 percent, however, I probably would not have been a standout. Those were all-star type games in which players were going one-on-one to attract the attention of the crowds. Again, that is not my style of play because I prefer team basketball.

The reason I attended the camps was because coaches and agents suggested I participate in order to prove I was over the injury and that it was not permanent.

Those performances, which I knew were substandard for me, caused some critics to downgrade my NBA chances. Larry Brown, the Pacers coach, was not one of those detractors. "People always focus on what guys can't do," he said. "With a kid like Bailey you have to look at what he can do." I had always tried to do a lot of things as a player and I think that is what he meant.

I am not fast, but neither were Larry Bird or Scott Skiles, a couple of other Indiana products who did well in the NBA. I am not tall, but there are players smaller than I who play well, play hard and play every night.

Still I did not know what to expect as the draft neared. I met with the Pacers and was told they would select me in the second round if I were still available. They did not know, nor did I, what other teams might do.

That was the year the draft was televised from the Hoosier Dome in Indianapolis where about 20,000 fans had gathered. Most of the players expected to be drafted early were in attendance. Eric Montross chose not to attend. I preferred to watch at my parents' home with them, Stacey, Courtney, Grandma and Papaw Bailey and Aunt Nancy Bailey.

We waited in suspense, like everyone else, as the teams slowly made their selections. I knew I was not going to be chosen early, certainly not in the first 10, but realistically I thought I might be chosen late in the first round. So I sat and waited, hoping to get picked, but not really caring by whom. Although I preferred the Pacers, I would have played for whomever picked me.

Some players I did not think were as good as I were drafted and I still waited. I knew not to be discouraged because pro basketball is a business and a player cannot take personally what does or does not happen to him. I realize teams select the players they think can help them the most.

The long wait ended when the Pacers made me the 44th pick of the draft. It was heartening to see almost each of the 20,000 people at the Dome erupt in a standing applause at the selection. It was good to know fans were delighted I would be part of the Pacers organization.

Donnie Walsh, the Pacers president, explained, "We think Bailey is a good player and we want to give him a chance to make it in the league. I can't think of a better coach than Larry (Brown) to help him."

Coach Brown added, "We took him because he has a chance to make the team. I look at what he has done in his career and I think he can be good."

* * *

It had been 12 years since I won that first MVP award at the 1983 national AAU tournament. The time had passed quickly.

No one goes through life without a few disappointments. One of the few regrets I had was that we did not win an NCAA championship, which would have been Indiana's sixth and Coach Knight's fourth. It was the only goal I had set that I had not realized.

I had dreamed of winning a state high school basketball championship. Our 1990 Bedford North Lawrence team did. I had dreamed of being Mr. Basketball. I had been in 1990. I had dreamed of playing for Indiana University. I had from 1990 to 1994. I had dreamed of being an All-American. I was in 1994.

I had played my entire career in Indiana. I had a great following. I had enjoyed the advantages basketball had given me. I had loved almost every moment. No one could ask for more.

I also had dreamed of being drafted by an NBA team. And now I had been selected by the Indiana Pacers. The rest would be up to me. I do know that I will play the game—as a professional or as a member of a church league team—for as long as my body will permit.

Basketball has allowed me to live a dream. I want to continue to live it.

A POSTSCRIPT

On September 23, 1994, three months after the NBA draft, I signed a contract with the Pacers. I had played with progressive pain in my knees since my sophomore year in high school and the Pacers management ordered surgery before the first practice started.

General surgery was performed on the left knee to repair cartilage damage. Reconstructive surgery corrected a tendon problem in the right knee.

I resumed practice late in the season, but did not play that season. My knees felt great, free of pain for the first time in years.

* * *

That fall I went into business, joining Randy Hawkins, whom I had worked for at Hoosier Auto Parts in college. We operate the Hawkins-Bailey Warehouse, a distributor of maintenance products as a service to coal mines, construction companies, stone quarries, factories and other concerns. My father, Wendell, now works for us.

* * *

I married Stacey Ikerd on August 12, 1995, in Bedford after a courtship of nine years.

* * *

My sister Courtney entered her sophomore year at Indiana University in the fall of 1995, living on campus after commuting from home as a freshman.

She and I continue to do what we can to help different social service agencies. I am involved with "Damon's Team," a group that raises corporate contributions which are used to type potential bone marrow donors.